GROWING
OLD-FASHIONED
ROSES

Barbara Lea Taylor

CASSELL

Dedication

To my mother – in love and admiration

They are not long, the days of wine and roses;
Out of a misty dream
Our path emerges for a while, then closes
Within a dream.

Ernest Donovan

Photographs by Barbara Lea Taylor, except for those on pages 33, 35, 36, 37, 38, 71, 76, 77, 78, 88, 89, 89, 91 (top), 93 (top), 94 by Geoff Bryant; 1, 4, 6, 9, 19, 21, 41 (bottom), 67 (top) by Gil Hanly; 64 by Juliet Nicholas; cover pictures, 46, 47, 50, 75 (top left) by Rosemary Thodey.

Care has been taken to get the colour in the photographs as accurate as possible, but with roses colours can vary even from flower to flower of the same variety.

Cassell Publishers Limited
Wellington House, 125 Strand
London WC2R 0BB

Copyright © David Bateman, 1996

First published in Great Britain in 1996
in association with
David Bateman Limited
Tarndale Grove, Albany Business Park, Bush Road
Albany, North Shore City, Auckland, New Zealand

Distributed in the United States by Sterling Publishing Co. Inc,
387 Park Avenue South, New York, NY 10016, USA

British Library Cataloguing in Publication Data
A catalogue record for this book is available from the British Library

ISBN 0-304-34850-3

Printed in Hong Kong by Colorcraft Ltd

Contents

'Mme Ernst Calvat'

Title Page: 'Crépuscule'

	Introduction	5
1	History	7
2	Landscaping with old-fashioned roses	
	Roses for all sites	10
	Roses for all seasons	14
	Roses for garden fragrance	16
	Companion plants	17
3	Cultivation	
	Selecting your roses	20
	Planting	22
	Nourishing	26
	Pruning	28
	Propagation	30
4	Pests and diseases	
	Pests	33
	Diseases	34
	Spraying	35
5	The old-fashioned roses	
	Species roses and close hybrids	36
	Gallicas	40
	Damasks	45
	Albas	48
	Centifolias	51
	Moss roses	53
	Chinas	56
	Portlands	59
	Bourbons	61
	Noisettes	65
	Rugosas	68
	Hybrid Perpetuals	71
	Teas and Hybrid Teas	73
	Climbing Teas and Hybrid Teas	76
	Hybrid Musks	79
	Shrub roses	83
	Shrub climbers	86
	Climbers and ramblers	88
	Bibliography and further reading	95
	Index	95

FOREWORD

The author's cottage full of old-fashioned roses.

IT IS 9.00 pm and I have just come in from the rose gardens. It is June, sultry and now gently raining after a hot day. It is the time when roses are at their wonderful best, their perfume hanging in the damp, warm, still air. 'Mme Alfred Carriere' is blushing even more than in the heat of the day and the subtle purple shades of 'Charles de Mills' are fresher and more intense than they were even an hour or two ago.

I set this scene only because it happens this way just once or twice through any rose season and sometimes we are far too preoccupied and busy to notice. It is during these very personal moments that a lifelong affinity with roses is brought into full focus and perspective, and an answer is found to the frequently asked question, "why old-fashioned roses?"

Everyone will have different reasons for their commitment to the heritage rose, but each of us who take pleasure from them will have consciously, or more likely subconsciously, experienced the very same moment in time with our roses or gardens of roses. It doesn't matter that I am writing this in England in June; in New Zealand in November that same idyllic moment will exist to consolidate what up to then may have been no more than a whim.

From her writings and descriptions of roses, I know that the author of this book has also experienced that moment with roses which cements a relationship with them. Those of us in the same club are the richer for Barbara Lea Taylor's writings, and those who are as yet not fully committed but seek that moment, will come much closer to finding it having read this book.

Peter Beales
Attleborough
England

INTRODUCTION

One comes back to old-fashioned roses as one does to music and old poetry.
A garden needs old associations, old fragrances, as a home needs
things that have been lived with.

Marion Page

'Old Blush'

IN THE preface to his book, *Down the Garden Path*, Beverley Nicholls explains that he must write it quickly 'for shortly I shall know too much . . . shall dilate, with tedious proxility, on the root formation of the winter aconite, instead of trying to catch on paper the glint of its gold through the snow as I remember it last winter, like a fistful of largess thrown over a satin quilt.'

When I wrote my first book about old roses, I thought I knew a lot about them. When I came to write this, my second, I realised how little I knew, and therefore the reader is still safe. If the agony is addictive and I ever write book number three, I shall discover how much there is still to learn.

Whereas my first book dealt with a small number of old roses, this one includes many more and describes them in greater detail. If in parts it appears lighthearted, that does not mean the subject is not taken seriously. But old roses are meant to lift the spirits, not to furrow the brow.

Document them how we may, chances are they will bloom on regardless, and continue to do so long after we are gone. Purists con-

sider roses to be 'old' only if they were bred before 1867 when 'La France', the first Hybrid Tea, was introduced. Along with many other rosarians, I have interpreted the word 'old' more liberally and included late-19th-century roses as well as some from the 20th century. I have had space to mention only a few. There are many, many more, of course. Catalogues of specialist nurseries often list more than a thousand, and every now and then another forgotten rose is rescued from an old garden.

In Part 1 of the magnificent series *Old Garden Roses*, (published in 1955) Sacheverell Sitwell wrote, 'There are, it need hardly be said, treasures still to be found and the list of old roses is not and never will be at its last page.'

We are fortunate to have old-rose enthusiasts who approach the rose in so many different ways, from the purely botanical to the unashamedly romantic, and all the degrees in between. The really lovely thing about gardening is that one never ceases to learn, nor loses one's capacity for delight.

Chapter 1

HISTORY

'Souvenir de la Malmaison'

ONE perfect long-stemmed clone of a rose, stiff in its plastic shroud, is definitely not my ideal.

In fact, a garden full of perfect, long-stemmed, modern roses would not do for me.

But a garden full of tumbling, arching, sprawling, rambling, cascading old-fashioned roses, rich as regency silk, delicate as tissue paper, soft and shiny as satin, fragile as butterfly wings, sumptuous and full-petalled, or wide-eyed singles, is another matter altogether!

So many modern roses, bred for fluorescent colours, a high peaked form, and a long flowering period, have lost their perfume in the process — and what little they do have

is not easily released. To have killed the scent in the rose is poor recompense for larger flowers and longer blooming. Scents trigger our memories. A waft of perfume can bring long forgotten places, people and emotions vividly into focus.

Old-fashioned roses, with their flat and quartered or loosely cupped blooms, exhale their fragrance freely and were designed for noses to sniff.

If you are a finicky gardener and get twitchy when your garden's not immaculate, then old roses are probably not for you. Stay with the pointy-headed ones, preferably standards. You can cut them back to a stick with a few knobs on top in winter, and nothing could be neater. But if you happen to be a romantic with a practical streak, it is easy to fall under the powerful spell of old roses, and when that happens, there is no escape.

Opposite: 'A garden full of tumbling, arching, sprawling, rambling, cascading old-fashioned roses . . .' ('Ballerina' in foreground).

'Mme Lauriol de Barny'

It is the beginning of a love affair that will last a lifetime — and there aren't too many of those about! These roses will give far more than they expect from you, and you will never be bored. Their beauty and fragrance will stay in your mind's eye through the long cold winters, and every spring and summer will be filled with new flowery pleasures.

Read the catalogues and the names will drip like poetry from the tongue: 'Tuscany', 'Reine des Violettes', 'Ispahan', 'Rose du Roi', 'Mme Legras de St Germain', 'Maiden's Blush', 'Mme Lauriol de Barny', 'Anne-Marie de Montraval', 'Prince Camille de Rohan', 'Celestial', 'Belle Amour', and so on. Many of the loveliest roses have French names simply because French rose breeders were particularly active and successful in the 18th and 19th centuries.

Roses have a history that overflows with passion and mystery. Rose fossils believed to be 35 million years old have been found in rocks in Europe, Asia and North America and we know that these prehistoric roses were five petalled flowers not very different from *R. eglanteria*, the wild 'Sweet Briar'. Certainly, prehistoric man would have been more interested in the fruit (hips) of the rose than its flowers.

The history of the rose is interwoven with human history and, through the ages, medicine, religion, literature and art have paid homage to the rose. A mere 4,000 years ago, a Minoan artist on Crete painted a picture of a single rose on a fresco that decorated the ancient palace of Knossos. Oil of roses is mentioned by the Greek poet Homer in the 9th century B.C. and when Sappho composed *Ode to the Rose* in the 6th century B.C., she called it the 'Queen of flowers'.

Rome, in its heyday, not only grew roses extensively, but imported shiploads from Egypt so the fragrant petals could be used for table and house decoration as well as for wreaths and crowns. One Roman, Heliogabulus, arranged to shower his dinner guests with rose petals, but so many were used that several of the guests suffocated.

In the 1st century A.D., the great naturalist Pliny (the elder) described the rose species known at the time. In Jerusalem in 1187, the sultan Saladin used 500 camel-loads of rosewater to purify the mosque of Omar after the expulsion of the Crusaders. In the Middle Ages, the rose was prized for its medicinal value, and just a few centuries ago, Shakespeare mentioned the rose repeatedly in his plays and sonnets.

To write about roses without mentioning the Empress Josephine would be like writing the history of Europe without mentioning Napoleon. Josephine had always been passionately interested in roses. After her divorce from Napoleon she retired to her estate outside Paris, La Malmaison, where she employed the best botanists, hybridists

Climbing roses add a colourful dimension to this formal garden. ('Alchemist' at left, 'Albertine' on the arches.)

and gardeners to create the Malmaison rose gardens. Because of Josephine, rose seeds and sometimes the botanists themselves were given safe passage between England and France all through the Napoleonic Wars. Also thanks to Josephine, all the most rare and beautiful roses flourished at La Malmaison, and in the 19th century, France became the leading exporter of roses in the Western world.

Chapter 2

LANDSCAPING WITH OLD-FASHIONED ROSES

'Buff Beauty'

THERE is no other genus of plant that can be used for so many different garden purposes as the rose. It would be possible to land-scape an entire garden with nothing but old-fashioned roses, using climbers, ramblers, shrubs, bedding plants, container plants and groundcovers.

Roses for all sites
Shrubs in borders and beds
Unlike modern Teas and Floribundas, which are basically bedding plants, many old roses make excellent shrubs. Species, Gallicas, Centifolias, Damasks, Albas, Chinas, Port-lands, Rugosas, some of the Teas and Hybrid Teas, and especially the Hybrid Musks, are inclined to form naturally attractive bushes. A lot depends on the individual rose, and in

the chapter describing the roses I have indi-cated their habits of growth. Many roses with bushy growth are more suitable for inclusion in borders as large shrubs rather than bed-ding plants, but may not have sufficient sub-stance for a shrubbery or to stand alone in grass.

Bourbons make large and wonderfully floriferous shrubs if the new shoots are pruned when they reach about 1.5 m and then pegged down in a horizontal position to encourage each shoot to flower along its entire length. The technique can also be used most successfully with some Hybrid Perpetuals and Centifolias.

To create an attractive shape, select the longest shoot first, remove about 45 cm of growth from the tip, then peg into the hori-zontal position. This should be done with black string attached to wire hooks which are pushed into the soil so that they cannot be worked free as growth develops and the plant is shaken by wind. This procedure can be repeated with all the longest growths and a mushroom pattern will develop.

A few of the canes should be cut short and retained to fill the centre of the plant so that there is no scarcity of bloom in this area. (See Diagram 1.) You need space for this but it is not difficult to do, and the end result is a delightful flowery mound.

Of course, there is nothing in the rules that says you can't use old roses for bedding. Choose those with moderate growth and a long flowering period. All good gardens are presumed to be the better for at least a nod to formality, and how better to do it than with a bed of massed roses surrounded by a low clipped hedge.

Specimens in grass

Roses growing unaccompanied and un-adorned in grass hold a special charm for me. Repeat-flowering, well foliaged roses planted as specimen shrubs on a lawn are superb. I have found that without competition they quickly become established and romp away to their heart's content. Hybrid Musks — particularly 'Buff Beauty', 'Penelope', 'Felicia', 'Cornelia' and 'Autumn Delight' — and the China rose, 'Mutabilis', are excellent varieties for this treatment.

Big shrub roses need support. One method is a tripod of rustic branches, painted wood, trellis or metal, depending on the degree of formality in your garden. Roses that hang their head, such as 'Buff Beauty', look their best arching from a tripod or a cage-like structure with four poles instead of three. Both tripod and cage need support bars at intervals between posts.

Neither of the above structures will encourage immaculate lawn mowing. If you use rustic supports for sprawling roses, do not be

prissy and spoil the effect by planting neat little rings of pansies at their base. Let the grass grow long enough for white daisies to show, and just claw it back a bit from the rose and its support. Shaven lawns are lovely in their place — a bowling green, for instance — but a bit daunting and unsettling in a tranquil, romantic garden.

Roses in woodland

If you have space for a woodland garden, the hardy, disease-resistant, easy-care Species and Rugosas are what you need. They will

Diagram 1: Pegging a rose

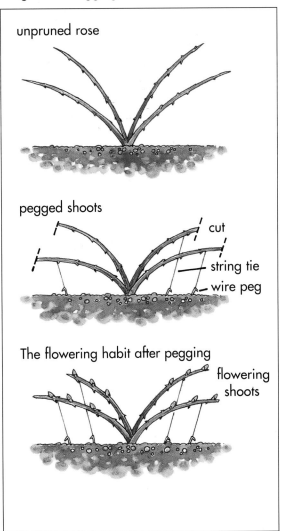

unpruned rose

pegged shoots

cut

string tie

wire peg

The flowering habit after pegging

flowering shoots

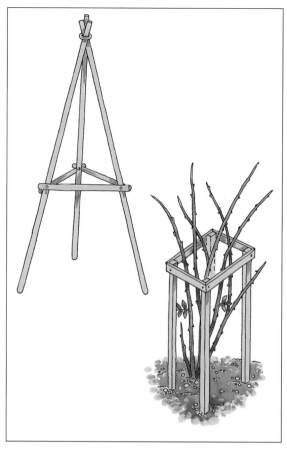

Diagram 2: Rose tripod and cage designed to support long canes

houses, however well designed, benefit from the softening effect of climbers, and old houses always look wonderful draped in roses.

If you are worried about accessibility for repainting walls, you can use a trellis for roses to climb and just hook the trellis to the wall. When you need to repaint, simply unhook the trellis and lay it, with its roses, flat on the ground. You could do the same with a frame around wires or plasticised netting. Alternatively, you can use plasticised expanding wires (green). Hook these to the base of the house and up under the eaves, and tie the roses to the wires.

Verandah posts and other pillars, pergolas, gazebos, arbours and arches all cry out for roses. Think about planting climbers and ramblers to scramble up trees. Many roses will grow well in the shelter of a tree, and although it may take a year or two before they get their heads into the light and begin

provide blooms and interesting foliage in spring and summer, and many will put on a brilliant autumn display of colourful foliage and hips.

Roses overhead

Someone remarked to me once that however small the surface, a garden is 4,000 miles deep, and that's a substantial property. I suppose the reverse applies, and on the tiniest piece of land you can go up. Presumably there will be house walls and fences to accommodate roses.

I should like to see every ugly fence in the land covered with roses. Think what a difference it would make to suburbia! There is a saying that 'doctors bury their mistakes and architects cover theirs with climbers'. New

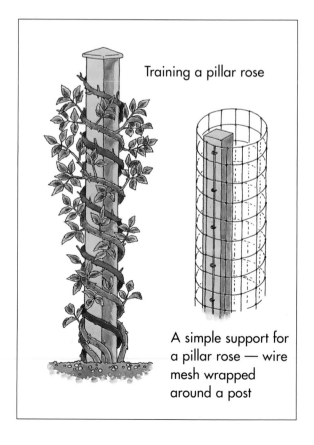

Training a pillar rose

A simple support for a pillar rose — wire mesh wrapped around a post

'Minnehaha'

to bloom, it is worth waiting for. Garlands of flowers trailing and looping against the dark background foliage of a tree are a charming sight which adds an extra dimension to the garden.

In time, given some of the more rampant varieties, you may get more rose than tree, so it is best not to choose a particularly ornamental specimen as host. Old trees that are no longer attractive but would be difficult to remove are ideal.

Roses in containers

Many old roses are perfectly happy in containers — oak half-barrels, large terracotta stone or concrete urns and pots — as long as they have good soil and free drainage.

Make sure the container has drainage holes. Shingle or broken pieces of brick or terracotta should be placed on the bottom. Immediately over this, place a layer of damp peat to stop soil blocking the drainage holes, then fill the container with good quality pot-

ting mix. The roses will need feeding in spring and summer, and the top 10 cm of soil should be renewed each year.

Smaller roses that are excellent in pots are: 'Grüss an Aachen', 'The Fairy', 'Anne-Marie de Montraval', 'Hermosa', 'Perle d'Or', and the ever-flowering little 'Paree' roses, low-growing cluster flowered roses which come in white, red and salmon-pink.

If your garden is the paved courtyard of a townhouse, it is better to leave spaces in the paving to plant roses, particularly near the walls for climbers. However, climbing roses can be grown successfully in large containers. I have grown climbers in half-barrels which reached second-storey windows and flowered well.

The absolutely essential thing for the success of container-grown plants is regular watering and feeding. Make sure that water gets right down to the roots of the plant, which should never be allowed to dry out.

Few plants cover archways as effectively as old-fashioned ramblers and climbers.

Ground-covering roses

Roses are not true groundcovers. They will not block out light and suppress weeds as effectively as some creeping plants and prostrate shrubs, but they can form impenetrable mounds and cover unsightly parts of the garden such as tree stumps and difficult banks. Roses will never become invasive.

If you have a bank to cover, nothing could be prettier than a rambler. I have used 'May Queen' for covering a steep bank in a hillside garden. It formed a dense thicket, kept its glossy leaves all winter, and there was always a flower or two to pick. 'Dundee Rambler' is another rose that will bridge gaps between terraces in a hilly garden.

'Sea Foam' is more of a shrub climber, but it is a lax plant and if left alone it will form a spreading mound. 'Macrantha Raubritter' can be used in the same way. 'Max Graf' is a Rugosa hybrid with prostrate growth and vigorous trailing shoots that will take root. Foliage is thick and glossy and flowers are silvery pink.

'Nozomi', which is sometimes used as a weeping standard, has many small single pink flowers and makes a dense plant, ideal for cascading. 'Snow Carpet' is really a miniature rose that spreads and hugs the ground. Each plant will eventually cover about 1 metre square. Flowers are small, double and creamy-white, followed by tiny bright hips in autumn. There are many other ground-covering roses to choose from, both old and new.

Roses for all seasons

It is a lot to ask from one plant — beauty of face and form, fragrance, good health, a long life and an elegant death! Yet it is possible to have all of these virtues in a rose, although in the end it will come down to a matter of degree.

A Gallica may give you just six weeks of glorious blooming — unstinting, extravagant and breathtaking. I can think of no better example than 'Charles de Mills' with its unforgettable flowers of such magnificence that perhaps six weeks is all we could bear! A rose like this might be considered worth a garden full of perpetual bloomers that are pretty enough but don't take our breath away by the sheer exuberance of their display.

On the other hand, the more I grow roses, the more I am inclined to demand from them. A pretty face is not everything.

More than a pretty face

Before you buy a rose, consider its habit of blooming. Will it bloom for six months of the year or will it bloom only in spring or in summer? If it is classed as 'recurrent', how quickly does it repeat bloom? Are there many weeks or months with no flowers at all? It is lavish or miserly with its flowers?

It is easy to be beguiled by a photograph of an exquisite rose, but perhaps (perish the thought) it was the only bloom that plant had all season! I have mentioned in the next chapter how important it is to see the bush in flower before you choose a plant.

You may even want to consider what the blooms look like as they die. Do the pathetic wizened corpses hang a long time on the bush? This probably doesn't matter too much if the rose will climb a tree or romp away in the grass with other shrubs, or if you are a dedicated dead-header. But if you intend to plant it against a wall, on a pergola or an arch, or near a door, it is worth bearing this in mind.

Single roses die beautifully. They fall petal by petal to reveal a crown of gold or amber stamens, but it does plumb the depths of decadence, I suppose, to judge our roses on how well they die.

Rose forms

Consider the bush itself. Is it naturally inclined to grow to a pleasing shape or are the canes thin and straggly, needing guidance and support? The blooms may be so lovely that this is a trivial point, but there are areas in a garden where it is nice to have a bush that will look after itself. The Gallica 'Duchesse de Montebello', for example, seems to have a happy knack of growing to a symmetrical pear-shaped bush, perfect for displaying its pink porcelain flowers. However, it flowers only once!

The Portland 'Jacques Cartier' is always well foliaged, with never a leaf out of place, and its blooms are perfectly framed. Foliage is important. All rose leaves are by no means the same. They can be all shades of green, russet and maroon, and a variety of shapes, including feathery and ferny. They can be lush and abundant; sparse, soft and downy; or smooth and shiny. Some provide better backgrounds for their blooms than others.

The Species *R. dupontii* displays pearly single blooms superbly set against big grey-green leaves. The full-petalled muddled

Old-fashioned rose forms

Button-eye

Quartered

Quilled

Cupped

Ruffled Rosette

Tea rose form

Single

Semi-single

blooms of the rambler 'May Queen' nestle in rich green leaves so glossy they almost sparkle in the sun. 'May Queen' will hold its leaves all year where winters are not too cold.

The Banksia rose and the Wichuraiana rambler, 'Albéric Barbier', are evergreen in temperate climates, which makes them ideal for covering woodsheds and unsightly structures. Remember that their hearts are in the country, so do allow them plenty of room. I wince when I see 'Albéric Barbier' pruned into submission and planted with other roses in a suburban garden. It's a charming rose but an exuberant one, and if you want it to run along a fence or cover an old building, it will do it before you can blink your eyes!

There are roses, particularly the Species and Rugosas, with foliage that colours magnificently in autumn. There are even a few roses grown as much for their foliage as their flowers. Two of these are *R. glauca* and *R. roxburghii*. *R. omeiensis pteracantha*, the Wing Thorn rose from Mt Omei in China, is grown primarily for its spectacular thorns. It has ferny foliage, but plant it where the light can shine through its enormous translucent fiery thorns. Don't plan on pruning!

R. alba hips

Rugosa roses have distinctive, handsome, deep-veined leaves that colour well in autumn. *Rugosa alba*, in particular, has leaves that are as butter yellow as autumn poplars, as well as fat, red, tomato-shaped hips — and probably a few flowers at the same time. Single-flowered Rugosas usually set magnificent hips.

Rosehips alone can be a feature of the autumn garden. The ferny foliaged, prickly *R. pimpinellifolia* 'Double Cream' has hips like fat blackcurrants. *R. moyesii* 'Geranium' has big, flagon-shaped orange-red hips. The long canes of *R. woodsii fendlerii* bow down under the weight of scarlet hips from base to tip. *R. foliolosa* has velvety-brown stems, flame-coloured foliage and small bright hips.

The popular Shrub rose 'Frühlingsgold' has masses of dark maroon hips on bronzy stems, and pale pink and pretty 'Fritz Nobis' is another that follows its flowers with an attractive display of hips.

'Thérèse Bugnet' is a tough Shrub rose bred to thrive in hard winters. Bright pink, perfumed double flowers are produced throughout summer, and in autumn her glowing flame-coloured leaves can rival the brightest specimen shrubs.

Roses for garden fragrance

Old-fashioned roses are always associated with fragrance. The appreciation of fragrance is very much a personal thing, but it is also dependent on the time of day and the weather. Very few roses can retain their perfume at high noon on a sunny day. Cool, cloudy days also inhibit fragrance. Roses smell their best on warm dry mornings. The makers of attar of roses have known for centuries that roses must be picked between 4.30 and 9.30 in the morning.

There is also a correct way to smell a rose: cup your hands over it, breath gently on it and sniff. I have heard of a nurseryman who, when told that a rose had no perfume,

'Jean Ducher' — centrepiece for a bed of fragrant lavender

would pick a bloom, put it under his hat, walk around with it for a few minutes, then hand the warm and fragrant rose to the customer.

A rose that is listed as 'fragrant' may not be noticeably scented to everyone. There are, however, roses that are powerfully and unmistakably fragrant. I defy anyone to deny the perfume of 'Mme Isaac Pereire', 'Kazanlik', 'Alba Semi-plena', 'Souvenir de la Malmaison', 'Blanc Double de Coubert', 'Maiden's Blush', 'Mme Legras de St Germain', 'Fantin-Latour', 'Lamarque', 'Frühlingsduft', 'Anna Pavlova' — and, of course, there are many, many more. If a rose is particularly fragrant, this will be mentioned in the relevant entry in Chapter 5.

Plant your heavily scented roses near windows and doors so that their fragrance can waft inside.

Companion plants

Nothing is prettier than an herbaceous border brimming over with old roses and complementary perennials, but it does mean hard work. When the English gardening greats, such as Vita Sackville-West, Gertrude Jekyll and others, said 'We made a garden', they meant that legions of humble gardeners were told what to do. (A slight exaggeration, perhaps, because these grande dames of gardening were not averse to a bit of grubbing in the dirt themselves, but they also had a great deal of help.)

However, apart from painting a charming picture, a carpet of perennials is the ideal summer mulch for old roses. Plant the old-fashioned cottagey kind, rather than the exotic beauties. Sprawly, informal perennials and annuals have the advantages of looking most at home when a bit dishevelled, and of suppressing weeds.

There are a host of plants to choose from and it really depends on your colour preferences. I feel that lavender is a must with

'Phyllis Bide'

roses, whatever their colour. The combination of their perfumes is delicious, and if your climate is mild enough to include Mediterranean lavenders (those with cone-shaped flowers), you will have flowers all year. However, the English lavenders (spiky heads of bloom in summer) are much more fragrant. A mixture of both types is a good idea. For a touch of formality, you can use *L.* 'Grey Hedger' for a quick silver-leafed hedge or edging that lends itself to clipping into neat hummocks.

Aquilegias (Granny Bonnets, Columbines or Doves Round a Dish) have an airy grace that complements roses beautifully. Left to themselves, they will seed and come up year after year in surprising places — and colours. Delicate pinks, whites and blues will eventually revert to a basic, but not unpleasant, maroon.

Clematis are ideal companions for climbers and shrub climbers, but make sure you choose non-rampant, summer-flowering hybrids. The most suitable are the smaller flowered *C. viticella*, *C. taxensis* and some of the *C. jackmanii* hybrids. These flower on the current season's growth and can be cut back hard after flowering. All dead stems should be removed from the rose, and the clematis will happily repeat its performance next year. You can have fun with colour combinations. Try a deep purple clematis threaded through buff yellow roses for a dramatic effect, or the luscious silvery-mauve double *C.* 'Belle of Woking' with plum-purple roses.

Companion planting warrants a book to itself and I have space here for the briefest of mentions. Have fun experimenting. Try anything that appeals to you. The idea is to enhance, rather than upstage, the roses. Combining colours in the garden is painting with a very broad brush and the nice thing about it is that if you don't like this year's creation, you can rearrange it completely next year.

Opposite: '. . . you can grow roses almost anywhere.'

Chapter 3

CULTIVATION

'Souvenir de St Annes'

THERE is no mystique about growing old roses. Modern roses grown for showing may need coddling but most older varieties are remarkably hardy, otherwise they would not still be with us. Very often these roses are the only survivors of abandoned and derelict gardens.

It is not practical to list roses for particular localities; there are too many variables, depending on the particular garden conditions. Old roses can cope with English winters and they can cope with heat; the rose gardens of India are world famous. There are wonderful old-rose gardens in many diverse soils and climates, and you can grow roses almost anywhere.

Selecting your roses

Before you buy a rose, it is sensible to see it growing. Check with gardening friends and the old rose section of your nearest botanical

gardens. Many specialist old-rose nurseries have elaborate display gardens and if you can possibly visit them, do so. You will then have a much better idea of the plant as a whole — blooms, perfume, foliage, habit of growth, height — and its possibilities in your garden. In fact, you will almost certainly get quite carried away, stay much longer and buy much more than you intended.

Early summer is the best time to see old roses in their prime, but flowering times will vary with the location and the weather. A preliminary telephone call to the nursery is a good idea.

If you cannot see the roses in the flesh, you will have to rely on catalogues and people like me. One golden rule to remember, though, is that your old roses will need more space than you think they will.

There are two ways of buying roses: as 'bare root' plants or in containers. Bare root

roses are usually ordered from the grower for delivery and planting the following season. Popular varieties need to be ordered early. If you can, it pays to choose and order in early summer for delivery the following autumn or early winter. The roses will arrive freshly dug from the growing fields, packed in a box with their roots in damp straw or shredded paper covered with plastic.

A good plant should have at least three strong shoots coming from the bud union

These Hybrid Musks ('Felicia' left foreground, 'Penelope' at rear) show the results of regular feeding and watering.

where the branches meet, although some old roses may have only two and make up for it as they grow. A plant with only one shoot, however, is of poor quality. There should be a well developed main root and a number of fibrous roots. It is vital to keep the roots damp. If they look dry, soak the plants overnight in a bucket of water.

'Heeling in' new plants

'Cornelia'

If you cannot plant your new roses immediately, you must 'heel' them in. This simply means digging a trench anywhere in the garden where there is reasonable soil, placing the roses in it a little apart, and then replacing the soil over the roots and the junction of the stem and new shoots, and pressing it down firmly with the heels. The plants don't have to be upright, as long as the roots are well covered with damp soil. If your roses arrive when it is pouring with rain and the soil is soggy, it will be more comfortable for all concerned if you heel them in temporarily. They can stay like this for weeks if necessary until you can plant them in their permanent homes — just make sure the roots stay damp.

Container-grown roses are sold at retail nurseries in spring and summer in black plastic bags or pots. These are usually well grown plants, often in bud or flower, so they give you a better idea of what you are getting. They are also more expensive. Bare root roses have time to establish themselves in the garden before their flowering period and, for me, they do rather better than the container-grown variety — or perhaps I simply find it more fun.

However, if you forget to order in advance or just happen to fall in love with some luscious rose flowering in a nursery when all you intended to buy were onion and lettuce plants, at least you have instant flowers and know precisely what you are getting.

Planting

While some of my rose-growing habits are definitely laissez-faire, I do believe that correct planting is vital.

Before you do anything else, you need to choose a spot where the rose can get adequate sunshine and nourishment. Even roses that tolerate shade will grow better if they have sun for at least half the day. Rugosas are capable of flourishing despite strong winds, but most roses grow better with some degree of shelter, particularly when they are young.

What they positively hate are wet feet. It is unkind and unprofitable to plant a rose where the soil is heavy and waterlogged. You can, of course, improve the soil by drainage and the addition of well rotted manure, peat and coarse sand. On the other hand, if your soil is almost pure sand, you will need to build it up with large amounts of organic matter, and also water frequently — or plant Rugosas.

It is important to remember that no rose likes to be put into another rose's bed. Never immediately replace one rose with another. Chances are that your new rose will succumb to 'rose sickness' because the soil will be contaminated with secretions from the roots of the previous plant. It will survive but it will never thrive. If you want to plant where roses have been, you must dig out a barrow-load of soil and replace it with soil from another part of the garden, for example from the vegetable garden. Alternatively, leave the soil for a season until it is clean again. You can plant perennials, annuals or other plants there in the meantime.

However, roses are not demanding beauties. Free-draining soil, sun, a reasonable amount of moisture, and shelter from strong winds are modest requirements considering the rewards.

If you plan to support the rose with some sort of structure, all the best books will tell you to have it in place before you plant so as not to disturb the roots. I'm sure this is a good policy if you intend to build a summerhouse, gazebo, pergola, arch or arbour, but I find it very awkward crawling around trying to plant a rose under a smaller support such as a tripod, wigwam or 'cage'. So go ahead and plant the rose unhindered, but try to put the support up quite soon.

Ideally, the soil should be well cultivated and enriched with old, well rotted compost (those last four words should be engraved on every gardener's heart) several months before you plant. But few of us are so well prepared and the chances are that we simply wander out into the garden with the new rose in one hand and a spade in the other. Do not despair. Just make sure the rose has a reasonable start by digging a hole much, much bigger than you think you need, and lining it with good soil from somewhere else in the garden. (Try the vegetable garden again and if it happens to be the pride and joy of another family member, blame the dog!)

'Roseraie de l'Hay' — one of the best of the hardy Rugosas.

Bare root roses

Make sure these do not dry out. It is a good idea to soak them overnight in a bucket of water before planting. Leave enough room in the hole for the roots of the rose to be spread out. I use well-soaked, good quality potting soil around the roots, but a mix of potting soil and peat would be equally suitable. Never put fertiliser of any kind in with a new rose.

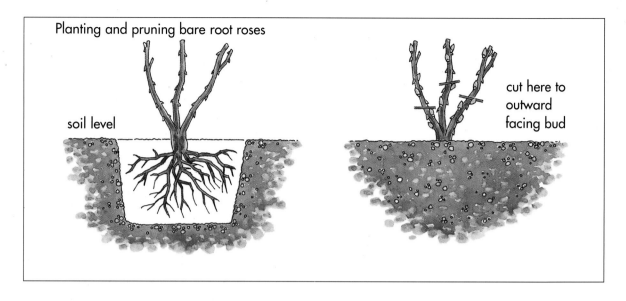

Planting and pruning bare root roses

soil level

cut here to outward facing bud

Place a few handfuls of potting mix in the hole to make a little mound in the centre. Position your rose on top of this so that it sits comfortably with its roots spread out, then spread a layer of potting mix over the roots. Fill in the hole in two or three stages, treading down firmly each time. Be judicious about this. The heavier the soil, the less you will need to tread it down. The rose should sit firmly, but not in hard, compacted soil.

Depth of planting is important. The bud union should be approximately 2.5 cm below the surface. The rose must be planted deep enough to be anchored against wind — no plant looks more unhappy than a rose rocking in its bed. A good covering of soil over the bud union will also protect a tender young plant from frost damage in a severe winter.

When your rose is safely planted, give it a bucket of water. Apply this slowly. Don't slosh it on all at once. Sprinkle a few handfuls of blood and bone on the soil around the plant and rake it in gently, or make five or six holes with a pencil and drop in a few grains of a long-term fertiliser such as Osmocote.

If you have removed the label, put a strong indelibly marked label beside your plant immediately. Yes, I know you are sure you will remember which rose it is but, believe me, the odds are against it, and chances are the rose will outlive you!

Now comes the hard part. Having planted your rose, you must proceed to demolish it; in other words, prune it hard. I know it seems cruel to hack into these frail defenceless plants, but we must not be squeamish! The reason for this pruning is to encourage all new shoots to grow from the base rather than the top, which would produce a leggy, awkward plant. Use sharp secateurs and prune to approximately 15 cm from the ground, just above a strong outward-facing bud, but at an angle facing the direction in which the bud is growing. Keep the rose moist but not waterlogged over the next few months and wait for your reward.

Container-grown roses

Planting procedures for these are basically the same as for bare root roses. Water the plant well the night before, or at least a few hours before planting. Place the rose, still in its polythene bag, in the prepared hole, then slit the side of the bag and remove it, trying not to disturb the roots. Make sure they have sufficient room in their new home, then proceed as detailed for bare root roses.

Container-grown roses for sale in spring

'Albertine', an old-fashioned rambler which climbs trees beautifully.

and summer will have been pruned already by the grower and therefore you do not need to prune them.

Roses to climb trees

Planting climbers or ramblers to climb trees is easy enough if done with care. Ideally, tree and rose should be planted together so that each can establish its own source of nourishment, but you need to start with a sizable tree to do this or the rose may outstrip the tree and have nowhere to go.

When planting a rose to climb an established tree, it is better to plant it a metre or more away from the trunk. Train the rose at an angle towards the tree along a stout stake or rope which is attached to the tree about 1.5 m from the ground. Tree roots will have impoverished the surrounding soil, so dig out a pocket where you intend to plant the rose and replace it with good soil.

Plant in the normal way but make very sure the rose is well watered for the first few months. Tree branches may shield it from rain and it will have to compete with tree roots for moisture. Bear in mind that the rose will tend to flower on the sunny side of the tree.

Transplanting

Even a large established rose can be successfully transplanted. Moving a plant during

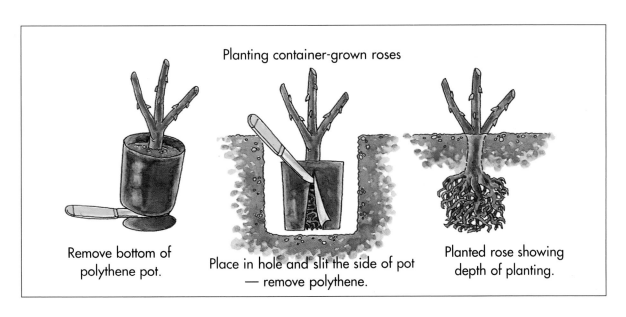

Planting container-grown roses

Remove bottom of polythene pot.

Place in hole and slit the side of pot — remove polythene.

Planted rose showing depth of planting.

its dormant period, which is in winter, is easy. Moving it in high summer is not recommended but there are times when it must be done. This is one time when the rose must be cut back hard — down to a few basic sticks, remembering to cut to an outward facing bud if you can.

Water the plant well for three days before you dig it out. Take time to dig out the rose carefully, damaging the roots as little as possible, although long tangles of fibrous roots can be trimmed before replanting. It may be quite impossible to dig out a very large, hoary old rose without considerable root damage. This may not matter too much. I have had ancient roses hacked out unceremoniously by builders and thrown on the ground in pieces. As long as each piece has a reasonable amount of root material, it will grow, although of course it is better to get the whole rose out if you can.

Dig a hole large enough to accommodate the root spread and plant it in the normal manner. Keep it well watered and shade it from hot sunlight for a week or two. Roses are amazingly resilient. I have never yet lost a transplanted rose and a lot of moving goes on in my garden.

Nourishing

If your soil is difficult, do not despair. Old roses are obviously survivors and will grow in any reasonable soil, although they do prefer it to be slightly acid. However, if you want them to grow well, it does pay to feed them.

Roses love humus. A soil rich in organic matter will give you healthy plants that bloom generously, and the best way to create this is to dig in well rotted compost and animal manures. There is nothing better than compost for roses, so if you don't already have a compost bin or a corner of the garden set aside for composting, think seriously about organising one. All household waste

'Alchemist'

except meat can go into it. By composting waste you can give back to the soil a measure of what you take out of it.

If you decide to use animal manures, well rotted horse, sheep, cow or pig manures mixed with well rotted untreated sawdust are effective. I am inclined to think horse manure is best. My grandfather bred horses — and grew magnificent roses!

Liquid fertiliser from seaweed and fish products is also excellent. If you live near the sea, you can collect your own seaweed, hose it down to remove as much salt as possible and leave it in a heap to break down before using it.

Commercial rose fertilisers, which contain a balanced mix of nitrogen, potassium and phosphorus, are a fail-safe option. Follow the manufacturer's instructions and do not be tempted to overfeed. The plant can assimilate only a certain amount.

Whatever you decide to use, roses should be fed well just as they are breaking dormancy in early spring, and again in midsummer for autumn flowers. Do not feed in autumn or you will encourage winter growth that cannot prosper.

I am not particularly keen on chemical fertilisers, but in the end, the way in which you feed your roses depends on the practicalities of supply and your own gardening philosophy. I have seen roses that flourished in poor soil on a diet of banana skins which contain calcium, magnesium, sulphur, phosphates, sodium and silica. A garden decorated with banana skins is not the prettiest sight, but they rot quickly if placed just under the soil. These same roses became stunted and sick when their banana skin diet stopped. Incorporating dried chopped or ground-up banana skins in your planting hole or potting mix is an idea well worth trying.

Water

This can be more important than food. Try not to let your roses dry out. Many mature old roses cope fairly well in dry conditions, but young plants and repeat-flowering roses need water. The most conscientious feeding programme will do nothing for your plants without water to deliver the food to the roots.

When you water, do it thoroughly. A good soaking once or twice a week is better than a casual sprinkling every day. If you water late in the day, keep the spray near ground level because wet foliage overnight encourages mildew. Early morning, before the sun is too hot, is best.

Mulching

Put your roses and companion plants to bed in late autumn with a good thick mulch of composted bark or pea straw, a protective blanket for the plants and a weed suppressant at the same time.

For easy gardening, top up the mulch in summer if necessary. At this stage, composted bark will look more attractive than pea straw. A summer mulch cuts down water stress because it reduces the soil temperature and keeps it from becoming compacted, which means that rain can reach plant roots more easily.

There is another way, of course. Weeds can be described as a living mulch. They add nitrogen to the soil, protect plants from erosion by rain, and provide homes for useful insects that prey on harmful bugs. And weeds are simply plants that are temporarily out of fashion! However, most of us would prefer not to have too many weeds, as they have a nasty habit of growing more lustily than our precious plants. An ongoing mulch of fine rotted bark looks attractive, smothers weeds and is generally pleasing. Remember, though, that this type of mulch does not feed the roses.

Pruning

Rosarians could debate methods of pruning until the cows came home. Pruning roses is no fun. I happen to believe that at least half the time it is a sort of self torture inflicted quite unnecessarily — a kind of Calvinistic gardening urge that tells us we ought to be out there doing penance for something, even if we can't remember what it is. Or perhaps there is something about hacking into bushes and putting a match to garden rubbish that uncovers some primitive instinct to slash and burn.

One of the nice things about old-fashioned roses, as opposed to modern, is that you do not prune them to a few pathetic sticks in winter. Apart from at planting time, most old roses are better not pruned at all for the first two or three years. They need time to build up a structure and establish themselves. You may then decide to leave them largely unpruned, except for the removal of dead wood, spindly shoots and shoots that are crossed or tangled. In other words, you may just give the bush a general tidy-up.

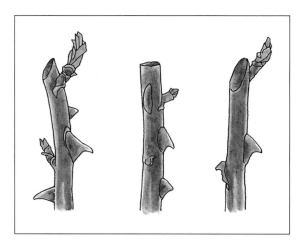

Pruning cuts: the one on the left is perfect. The cut in the middle is too stubby and too far removed from its new eye. The one on the right cuts too sharply into new growth. Make your cuts on a 45 degree angle, about 6 mm above a swelling bud eye.

If bushes get too leggy or sprawly, they can be cut back by reducing long side shoots by a third or more, but there is no great universal law that demands yearly pruning unless you are growing roses for exhibition.

When you do need to prune, make sure you do so at the correct time. Sharp secateurs are essential for the welfare of the roses — and strong gloves for your own well-being. Slip-on protective armlets are helpful, too. Prune just above an outward facing bud eye, making a clean cut at a 45 degree angle. Having said that, I have friends with wonderful roses who cut them back with hedge clippers when the need arises.

Once-flowering roses should be pruned as soon as possible after flowering, if you feel they need tidying or you wish to keep the bush within certain limits. I find that Gallica roses in particular benefit from cutting back immediately after flowering. They look better for it and they will be stronger next season because they will put out fresh new growth which has time to mature before winter.

Repeat-flowering roses can be pruned just before new growth begins, usually in late winter. If you wait too long, you will have to remove a few well-grown new shoots, but early pruning leaves the rose open to frost damage. You know your own climate best.

Climbers

With climbing roses the initial emphasis should be on training. For optimum flowers, the strong young canes must be trained as near to a horizontal position as possible. Bending the branches makes the plant send up flowering shoots all along the branches instead of flowering just at the top. Some of these side shoots can be tied to whatever you are using for support, such as a trellis or wires, so that the rose will spread upwards as well as sideways.

Pruning consists of shortening the side shoots by approximately two thirds each

'Céline Forestier'

year, and removing any old and unprofitable canes from the base as the plant matures.

Ramblers

Rambling roses are often used more informally for scrambling into trees or covering arbours and gazebos, in which case it is better to leave them unpruned for a year or two to let them become established. After this, prune to keep them within bounds and to remove old and dead wood.

Remember that many ramblers flower only once in a season, and if you choose to prune them, it should be done immediately after flowering. Because they flower on wood produced the previous season, if you wait until winter to prune you will cut away the coming season's flowering wood.

Climbers and ramblers growing high into trees are almost impossible to prune and they seem to get along very well without it, doing as Nature intended and gradually replacing old wood with new growth.

Deadheading

As you will have gathered, I am far from a manic or even a moderate pruner, but I am a conscientious deadheader. If you remove a spent flower before hips start to form, new flowers will be produced. The plant will continue to try to produce seed and in the process must flower again.

When you remove a dead rose, cut the stem just above the first proper bud-eye above a five-leafed branchlet. Done correctly, deadheading is a continuous summer trimming task. It can be a bit tedious if you have a lot of roses. (It is usually too difficult to deadhead roses up trees but they are probably once-flowering anyway.) Vita Sackville-West kept her secateurs tucked in the top of one of her knee-high gardening

Correct dead-heading cut for roses

boots but few of us are so elegantly shod in the garden. The best that most of us can do is to make a habit of picking up our secateurs every time we go into the garden.

The late Sir Humphrey Brooke, who died in 1988, grew the most magnificent roses at Lime Kiln in Suffolk. The soil is almost entirely inhospitable chalk surrounding an abandoned quarry, hence the name, yet his roses flourished and grew to unbelievable sizes. Sir Humphrey's method was to plant them in enormous holes and give them a start with good soil. After that they were left to fend for themselves. They were never pruned and no sprays or artificial fertilisers were ever used. A plant of 'Souvenir de la Malmaison', which has reached tree-like proportions, is said to be the largest in the world.

The last words on pruning have to be 'prune any way that works for you'. Some rosarians prune regularly, others not at all except to remove dead wood. The most important thing when you do prune is to make sure it is at the correct time of year.

Propagation

Growing roses from cuttings and layering are the methods of propagation most often used by the home gardener.

Roses from cuttings

Gertrude Jekyll wrote: 'They are much longer lived, they give more bloom more continuously, and they throw up no troublesome suckers. Grafted plants may be best for the production of show blooms, but the bush . . . is out of the category of beautiful things in the garden, whereas own root roses . . . fulfil their best purpose as true garden plants.'

Growing roses from cuttings is immensely satisfying. The gardener feels almost like a proud parent, and exchanging cuttings with friends is an economical way of acquiring new roses for the garden.

Commercially-grown roses are propagated by a process called 'budding'. This involves taking a bud — not a flower bud, but a growth bud — from the required rose and inserting it in the stem of a strong growing 'stock' rose, often a *multiflora.*

Occasionally, suckers will grow from the host 'stock' rose and these must be removed. They are usually sappier and have a different leaf. You can easily identify an unusual shoot as a sucker by digging carefully and finding the bud union where the rose has been grafted onto the root-stock. If the shoot comes from below this, it is a sucker from the root-stock. It is better to rip it off cleanly rather than try to remove it completely with secateurs.

This cannot happen with cutting-grown roses. Another advantage is that they withstand wind better, and if they are blown down, the original root-stock is there to send up new shoots.

Taking cuttings is easy. Getting them to grow is slightly more difficult. While it is possible to strike cuttings in summer, hardwood cuttings taken in autumn have the best chance of success. Take your sharp secateurs and choose a branch that has flowered: a branch from the current season is ideal. Old growth does not root easily and soft new growth is likely to wilt and die. Cuttings should be healthy, severed at a joint, or taken from the mid-section of the branch. Ideally, they should contain three or four growth buds and be approximately the thickness and length of a pencil, but smaller cuttings can do well as long as they have enough growth buds.

Cut on a 45 degree angle immediately below a growth bud. Some experts suggest removing thorns and all the leaves, while others like to leave the top two leaves. I don't think it matters all that much.

If you take cuttings from a climber which also has a bush form, be sure to take them from a climbing shoot or your cutting-grown rose may revert to a bush.

Place the cuttings in water immediately unless you have already brewed your willow tea. I always place cuttings in willow tea overnight before I plant them. (Sometimes I have left them for much longer with no ill effects.)

Willow tea

To make this excellent concoction, find a willow tree and cut off a few pieces of supple, green end shoots and leaves. You can put these in a blender with water and make a thin green soup, or you can simply chop them up and put them in a jar of water with your cuttings.

If you have no willow, do not despair. Willow trees contain salicylic acid, a substance used in aspirin. One aspirin dissolved in a litre of water will do the same job as willow tea.

Of course, you can use a commercial rooting hormone if you wish, although these are believed to have a limited shelf life and who knows how long they have sat in the shop before you bought them?

Potting up cuttings

Sharp river sand is a good potting medium. Put the sand in a pot and make sure that it is

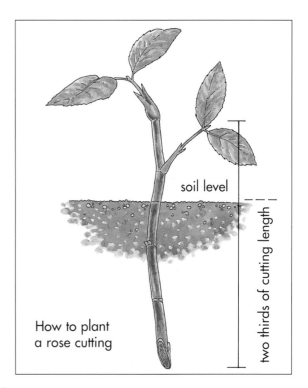

soil level

two thirds of cutting length

How to plant a rose cutting

well soaked. Plant your cuttings with at least two growth buds under the surface, which usually means that half to two thirds of the cutting is covered. They are happier in family groups (don't ask me why, but it happens!), so plant cuttings of the same variety close together. Keep your cuttings in dappled shade, and moist but not soggy.

By spring, the cuttings should begin to root and by the following autumn you should have small plants ready to be carefully placed in their permanent positions, or in larger pots.

Having said all this, you can simply poke the cuttings in a corner of the vegetable garden and have reasonable success with many roses. Don't forget to label them, though. I have heard, and it sounds logical, that the perfect place to grow cuttings is under the parent bush, given reasonable soil, but you cannot do that with a new rose.

Layering

This is a useful, old-fashioned method of propagating roses with pliable canes that are inclined to trail on the ground or can be easily persuaded to. Early spring is the best time to try layering.

Select a healthy young cane that has flowered the previous season, bend it down to the ground and make a shallow indentation in the soil at the point of contact so that part of the cane is covered. Then peg it down with a wire hook and cover it with a rock or two for good measure. It helps if you scrape the underside of the cane with a knife and peg it down at about 30 cm from the tip.

Keep the soil moist for a month or two, and when you see new growth appearing from the tip, you will know that roots have developed. You can then cut the cane from the parent plant and trim it back to relieve stress on the new roots. It is best not to move your new plant until the dormant season.

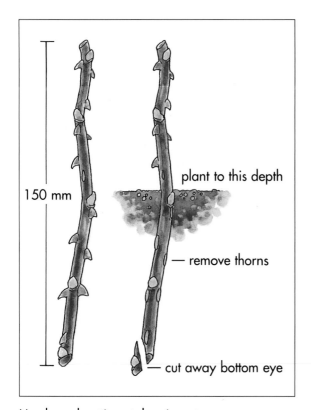

150 mm

plant to this depth

— remove thorns

— cut away bottom eye

Hardwood cuttings taken in autumn

Chapter 4

PESTS AND DISEASES

Aphids

Red mites

THERE are those who believe that any rose that can't make it without sprays is a wretched weakling and not worth bothering about. There have been in the past, are now, and probably ever will be many roses that are fashionable for a few years and then disappear because of their susceptibility to disease. Sometimes they are simply superseded by roses that are similar but better. It follows, then, that the old-fashioned roses we grow today are hardy survivors and deserve a little effort on our part to grow them at their best.

Roses grown in good conditions have a head start, but there are seasons when aphids, black spot and mildew can descend on the best of gardens. Whether you use chemical sprays depends on your gardening philosophy. I am not particularly happy about using them, but I do if I have to. The older I get and the more I learn about gardening, the less I'm inclined to be dogmatic, and gardening is 50 per cent magic anyway.

I can suggest choices but you must do what feels right for you.

Pests

Aphids

Apart from sucking the life out of the plant, aphid damage done while a shoot is forming can result in deformed leaves resembling peach 'leaf curl'.

There is an old belief that garlic or even garlic chives planted around roses keeps aphids away. The theory is that the roses ingest a substance from the garlic that aphids just can't stand. I have tried this method with doubtful results. For dedicated organic gardeners there are various mixtures which do work, but they need to be applied frequently. The following is an old-fashioned remedy that I'm sure would instantly demolish any insect up to and including the African rhinoceros beetle!

Organic rose spray for insects

Chop up a handful of garlic bulbs and six strong onions, then put them in a blender with half a cup of cayenne pepper. Bring this mixture to the boil in a big pot over an *out-side* burner. Boil for 5 minutes, let stand for 15 minutes, then strain. Use 1 tablespoon of this devil's brew to 4 litres of water. Be careful not to let it come in contact with your skin and good luck!

If you prefer not to do things the hard way, a simple method which does seem to work is to foliar feed every two or three weeks with liquid seaweed or fish fertiliser.

If you don't have too many roses, there is always 'digit control' or 'scrunching', which simply means that you strip the little horrors off with your fingers and 'scrunch' them to death in the process: a pleasant occupation for a summer evening!

Red spider mite

In warm areas, red spider mite can be a problem, usually in late summer. The mites are barely visible to the naked eye and often have a good hold before you realise they are there. Foliage becomes paler and eventually falls off. You need to look closely at the underside of leaves to detect the tiny mites and a tracery of webbing. Use a spray which incorporates a miticide immediately, and in winter use a good clean-up spray. (See Winter spray programme — page 35.)

White scale

This is most often seen on the mature wood of old established plants, particularly climbers. The pest that causes this unsightly scale has a flying stage and can spread to new bushes. The best method of control is thorough drenching with a clean-up spray in winter.

There are several good commercial sprays that will control both insect pests and fungal diseases. Most effective are the systemic sprays which enter the plant tissue.

Diseases
Black spot

This disease is identified by the blackish spots which appear on the leaves and spread rapidly until the leaves turn yellow and fall, leaving a defoliated, weakened bush. When the first black spot appears, I tend to forget all about organic gardening and reach for the spray to drench both stems and foliage, particularly newly emerging leaves. You may need to spray at fortnightly intervals on some susceptible roses.

Collect and burn all fallen leaves. If infected leaves are left at the base of the plant, spores of the disease will multiply, ready to attack the rose again next season.

Check that the affected roses are adequately fed and watered. Black spot is unsightly but rarely fatal and most old roses bloom on regardless.

Powdery mildew

This attacks leaves and buds, covering them with a greyish-white powdery mould which can quickly spread over the whole plant. Some roses are particularly susceptible. Powdery mildew appears most often in late summer or autumn when the main flowering period is over. Warm days followed by cold nights seem to be a catalyst. If you water your plants in the evenings, water the ground only and do not wet the foliage.

A mixture of 1 teaspoon of baking soda and 1 teaspoon of Sprayfix (or another spray adherant) added to 2 litres of water will control mildew, but you need to repeat this spray weekly.

Downy mildew

This is not common, but can occur in districts where humidity is high. Leaves develop purplish-red to dark brown irregular spots and eventually turn yellow and fall. Purplish-black

Black spot   Rust   Powdery mildew

areas develop on stems, and infected buds die. Use an appropriate fungicide to control.

Rust

Tiny orange spots appear on the underside of leaves and often go unnoticed until yellow blotches, which later turn black, appear on the upper surfaces. This is a serious disease that can spread quickly. Spray promptly, making sure the spray gets on the underside of leaves, and remove and burn all infected leaves. Some roses are particularly susceptible and you will have to decide whether or not they are worth keeping.

Spraying

Rather than list sprays for particular problems, I suggest consulting your local nursery for the spray best suited to your specific problem. There are now all-purpose fungicides available that are capable of controlling the three major problems of black spot, rust and mildew — and newer, more effective sprays appear on the market each year.

Having selected your spray, use it strictly as directed. *More is not better*. Never spray in hot sunshine or you risk leaf scorch and, of course, never spray when it is windy. The best time to spray is in the late evening when you are less likely to harm useful insects such as bees, and the spray will be more easily absorbed during the night.

Do take sensible precautions. Wear old clothes that cover your arms and legs and wash them afterwards. Cover your head, and wear a simple mouth and nose mask, which you can buy cheaply at a chemist. Take a shower when you have finished.

Perhaps all this isn't necessary if you have two roses in containers on the patio, but it is a very necessary precaution if you are dealing with a lot of the plants.

Winter spray programme

I am a firm believer in a good winter clean-up spray to destroy over-wintering spores of fungal diseases, scale, and eggs of aphids and mites. Done correctly, you should be able to greet spring with healthy roses.
1. At the beginning of winter, spray with lime sulphur. This is a defoliant as well as a clean-up spray and will ensure that your roses are dormant in winter. Drench bushes and surrounding soil. Rake up and burn all leaves.
2. In 3-4 weeks time, spray with a mixture of copper oxychloride and horticultural oil at winter strength. Drench the bushes and the surrounding soil. Repeat this spray after 3-4 weeks, not before.

Roses that have had any of these diseases should be watched carefully for any reappearance of symptoms the following season, and sprayed promptly and regularly with the appropriate deterrent.

Chapter 5

THE OLD-FASHIONED ROSES

R. banksiae alba plena 'White Banksia'

SPECIES ROSES AND CLOSE HYBRIDS

SPECIES roses are considered to be the original wild roses from which all later hybrids evolved. Initially, they would all have been five-petalled singles. This section will deal with a few of the species and their hybrids, many of which are still grown often as much for their beauty as garden shrubs as for their flowers. Sometimes, but by no means always, the flowers are quite insignificant.

These are roses for the connoisseur. After we have had our fill of the rich and voluptuous, we may find a quiet enjoyment in the simplicity of the species. They are often excellent for landscaping, many of them making very big shrubs and climbers, flowering only in spring but coming into their own in autumn with burnished foliage and bright hips. There is space to list only a few

of these roses and their near hybrids. For convenience and brevity, I have also included some *Pimpinellifoliae* ('Scotch' or 'Burnet' roses) in this group.

***R. banksiae alba plena* White Banksia Climber (1807)**   This rose is named for Lady Banks, wife of the naturalist Sir Joseph Banks, who did much for the planning of Kew Gardens in London and in the process dispatched a Scottish gardener, William Kerr, on a plant-hunting expedition to China. Foreigners were not welcome and plant-collecting as such was impossible. Kerr did manage to buy plants from the famous Fa-Tee nursery and ship them back to England. One of the few to survive the journey was the double white Banksia rose.

A vigorous and thorn-free climber, this rose has draped many a verandah and covered many a farm shed with its clusters of small white flowers. Some say it smells of violets but it doesn't to me.

R. banksiae lutea Yellow Banksia Climber (1825)   This was imported a little later than the White Banksia, from the same Chinese nursery by John Dampier Park, also from Kew, and is the more commonly grown variety. It romps away, covering anything in its path with its shiny leaves and thornless stems. In spring it is a mass of cascading clusters of fluffy butter-yellow flowers.

The woodshed behind my 1850s cottage has disappeared beneath a yellow Banksia planted perhaps 100 years ago. It's a glorious sight in spring, but don't let its rampant habit put you off. Because it has no thorns, the rose is easily controlled, although for maximum flowers it is better to plant it where it can have its way.

R. bracteata The Macartney Rose (1793)   Introduced from China by Lord Macartney, this is a beautiful rose with large, silky single white flowers bearing a bright coronet of golden stamens, set amidst glossy leaves. It makes a large shrub or moderate climber and has wicked hooked thorns very much like those of its more popular offspring, 'Mermaid'. Keep it for the woodland or shrubbery.

R. brunonii Himalayan Musk Climber (c.1822)   Clusters of small white single blooms in summer are deliciously Musk-rose scented. Big, attractive grey-green leaves and a mass of tiny orange hips add to its charms.

Canary Bird (c.1990)   Long arching branches on a big graceful shrub are covered for most of spring with quite large canary-yellow single flowers. Leaves are dark green and fern-like.

R. canina Dog Rose (ancient)   This ancient, hardy European wilding has spread far and wide and decorated country lanes for centuries. Late spring flowers are simple, lovely pink and white singles with prominent yellow stamens, followed by orange hips rich in Vitamin C. Robust, thick and thorny, it was once referred to as 'The Dog Rose'

R. banksiae lutea 'Yellow Banksia'

because it was believed that a cure for hydrophobia, a disease commonly caught from rabid dogs, could be made from its roots.

R. dupontii (1817)   I wouldn't be without this rose. The big, sweetly scented, perfectly symmetrical, single flowers are white with the faintest blush at the edges of the petals, and a coronet of golden stamens in the centre. The bush can grow very large — mine must be at least 3 m by 3 m and is currently

'Canary Bird'

working on climbing an apple tree. Leaves are soft, grey-green and plentiful. Flowers begin in late spring and continue through December. Autumn brings lots of little bright hips, so this is altogether a most satisfactory garden shrub.

R. eglanteria Eglantine Rose or Sweetbriar (ancient) Shakespeare wrote about this sweet wild rose of the hedgerows. It grows to an arching shrub and the flower is a pink single which appears briefly in summer. The attraction lies in the fragrance of its foliage, not its flowers. When the leaves are crushed or brushed in passing, or after a shower of rain, they release a delicious fresh perfume a little like green apples. The plant's winter hips have a high Vitamin C content and used to be gathered to make rosehip syrup.

R. fedtschenkoana (1868) Single white flowers with tissue-paper petal and an innocent charm bloom all summer on a dense shrub with noticeably glaucous, feathery foliage and a spreading, arching habit of growth. Bristly, bottle-shaped hips are tomato-red in autumn. This rose looks good in a shrubbery or wild garden and is named after its Russian discoverer, Olga Fedtschenkoana.

R. foetida bicolor Austrian Copper (c.16th century) A brilliant glowing jewel of a rose, this will light up the garden. Big, single, poppy-like flowers are a dazzling orange-flame with yellow stamens and a dark eye. It occasionally reverts to its yellow parent, *R. foetida*, and you get yellow and flame flowers on the same bush — a big prickly bush that grows to 2 m by 2 m. This is an important rose because it is the ancestor of all the modern bicoloured Hybrid Teas.

R. fortuniana (1850) Thought to be a natural cross between *R. banksiae* and *R. laevigata*, this plant has smooth thornless stems and almost evergreen leaves which resemble *R. banksiae*, but its growth habit is less hardy and more moderate and I find that it is not quite as free with its flowers. However, the creamy muddled double blooms are charming in spring.

Geranium (1938) Raised at Wisley by the Royal Horticultural Society, Geranium is the most popular seedling of *R. moyesii*, which was discovered in China in 1890. Velvety single flowers are Chinese-lacquer red with creamy stamens, and are followed by glistening, flagon-shaped autumnal hips. The plant is angular and thorny, but the brilliant flowers would light up a dark shrubbery.

R. glauca (previously R. rubrifolia) (prior to 1830) Named for its grey-green leaves and stems with plum-purple overtones, this is a rose grown for its foliage. The flowers are insignificant pink singles with a white centre, but they sit beautifully in the foliage and have a simple charm. Foliage colours well in autumn, accompanied by bunches of bright hips.

R. helenae (1907) This is a vigorous thorny climbing rose with glossy leaves and a superb display of big hydrangea-like heads of single, creamy-white, scented flowers in midsummer and small, bright red hips in autumn. Try growing it up a tree. Discovered in China by plant-hunter E H Wilson, this rose was named for his wife.

Kiftsgate (1954) A sport of *R. filipes* found

LEFT: *R. helenae*   RIGHT: *R. foetida bicolor*

at Kiftsgate Court in Gloucestershire, this wildly enthusiastic climber could probably envelop a suburban garden (and the suburb as well!), but it is lovely if you have the space. Huge, scented, cascading panicles of creamy-white single flowers with yellow stamens appear in midsummer, followed by lots of little red autumnal hips. This rose is wonderful in the woodland garden, but you may have to rescue the trees.

***R. laevigata* Cherokee Rose (1759)**   Big, single white flowers with yellow stamens are gorgeous garlanding a tree in spring. Growth is vigorous in temperate climates, but it does need a sheltered position to do really well. It has plentiful, shiny, dark green leaves and hooked thorns. This rose has become naturalised in the southern states of the United States of America since arriving there from China, and it is the state flower of Georgia.

***R. longicuspis* (1915)**   The species *R. mulligani* is so similar that it is often sold as *R. longicuspis*. A rampant climber, it will cover sheds and trees with its glossy foliage, which is almost evergreen. Big cascading corymbs of single white flowers appear in spring, followed by small orange hips in autumn. Hardier than Kiftsgate, this is the rose that makes you catch your breath in the famous White Garden at Sissinghurst.

Mermaid (1917)   This *R. bracteata* hybrid is an evergreen climber that flowers all year, and although there may be few blooms in winter, even one is enough to delight. Flowers are single, lemon-yellow with brown stamens, and enormous — up to 15 cm across — and they do have a wave-washed, undulating air. Once established, the plant is vigorous and viciously thorny. I once read an English catalogue that advised planting it 'to keep out animals and the public'. If you have boundary fences where you want to do just that, bearing in mind that it is also evergreen, Mermaid is the rose for you but good luck if you choose to prune!

***R. roxburghii plena* Chestnut Rose (1814)**   Even if you did not recognise this as a rose, you would be inclined to grow it as a handsome shrub. It has fresh green, fern-like foliage, buff-coloured bark that flakes, chestnut burred hips, and the most exquisite crepe paper scalloped frills of flowers — pale pink frills on the outside, decreasing in size and becoming deep pink in the centre. This rose is well worth having and extremely hardy.

GALLICAS

It was the 18th-century Swedish botanist, Carl Linnaeus, who came up with the name *Rosa gallica* because he believed that the species originated in France. As all of us who have struggled to remember botanical names will know, Linnaeus used Latin to classify his plant species, and 'Gallica' is the old Latin name for France.

The true beginnings of this most ancient family of roses are lost in the mists of time. We know it was cultivated and used as a religious emblem by the Medes and Persians more than 1,000 years before the birth of Christ. Early Greeks and Romans grew it for its medicinal qualities. Roman doctors took it with them on military campaigns, often planting it in their fortified camps where its toughness ensured its survival. No monastery garden would have been complete without it. Certainly *R. gallica* was grown for its medicinal qualities, but it was also valued for its beauty and the sheer pleasure of its perfumed petals, which held their fragrance even when dried.

The original wild species *R. gallica* seems to have been a deep rosy-purple single on a smallish upright prickly shrub. Because it seeded readily and the plants suckered and formed thickets, it not only survived but spread throughout Asia Minor and Europe.

In the Middle Ages, a highly scented semi-double variety we know as *R. gallica officinalis* was so popular for lotions, potions and powders that it was known as 'The Apothecary's Rose' and became the centre of a thriving industry at Provins near Paris.

In 15th-century England *R. gallica officinalis* became the red rose of Lancaster in the Wars of the Roses. The 16th-century herbalist, Gerard, grew it in his garden and listed it as *R. rubra*, the red rose, but the word 'pink' was not used as an adjective until the 18th century.

Elizabethan households regularly used Gallica and Damask roses in the preparation of conserves, puddings, syrups, jellies, soothing waters and, of course, potpourris for sweetening the air, which must have needed it badly in the days of no plumbing and little bathing!

The Gallica influence is evident in many of the roses introduced over the succeeding centuries and the Gallica hybrids we grow today have come a long way from that simple species rose of long ago. French hybridists were particularly busy in the first part of the 19th century when many of the Gallicas we grow today were introduced. Frilled, quilled, ruffled and quartered, with colours ranging from the palest shadow pink to hectic crimson-purple, or splashed and striped with a mixture of the lot, they can be both rubies and amethysts, vibrant and moody at the same time, but never boring.

These luscious roses of ancient lineage have not been bred to flower 'perpetually'. A spring and early summer display is all you'll get from most of them, but it will be a flowering to remember.

Gallicas are a hardy bunch not bothered by the dreaded black spot. They do mildew a bit in late summer, but by then their blooms have gone and it is a good idea to cut the plant back so that it can grow good new wood before winter. Gallicas, like other once-flowering roses, flower on the preceding year's wood. If you choose to prune, it must be done as soon as possible after flowering. If you leave it too late, you will cut off next spring's flowering growth.

***R. gallica officinalis* The Apothecary's Rose** We can still grow this heavily scented ancient rose. Deep pink to light red, loose semi-double flowers with prominent yellow stamens cover a shrubby upright bush that grows to little more than 1 m.

***R. gallica versicolor* Rosa Mundi** Striped and splashed as if a pale pink rose had been

Rosa Mundi

dipped in raspberry juice and shaken, the petals of Rosa Mundi have been compared to striped Regency silk. A sport of *R. gallica officinalis*, and identical except for the colouring, this rose was probably brought to England by returning Crusaders. Some people believe that Rosa Mundi simply means 'rose of the world' because it grew so freely. However, legend has it that Rosa Mundi was named after a 12th-century beauty, Rosamund de Clifford, mistress of Henry II.

Henry's wife was the formidable Eleanor of Aquitaine, who cornered Rosamund in the palace maze and gave her the choice of a speedy exit from the world by poison or a knife. Rosamund chose poison and presumably went home and died. The grief-stricken Henry picked a pretty, pink striped rose that grew wild in the hedgerows and ordered that it be named after her and that each year on the anniversary of her death, her grave at Godstow Nunnery in Oxford should be covered with Rosamund's rose.

Alain Blanchard (*R. centifolia* x *R. gallica*) (1839)   A beautifully composed rose, semi-single, with a double layer of petals that open wide to show long golden stamens. Crimson-purple petals are dappled with pink, and fade to violet as the flower ages. Growth is dense and bushy.

Anaïs Ségalas (1837)   A fragrant, flat and immaculately frilled rose, cerise purple fading to rosy-violet and finally lilac-grey as

'Anaïs Ségalas'

'Charles de Mills'

death approaches — and, of course, all of these shades are on the bush at the same time. It flowers early in scented profusion. A sturdy, suckering bush.

Belle de Crécy (before 1848) Raised in the gardens of Madame de Pompadour at Crécy, and a perfect memorial to a lady of sophisticated taste, 'Belle de Crécy' has been described as 'a scented breath of the perfumed voluptuousness of pre-war France' by a writer who may have confused the lady with the rose! But the rose is exquisite. Layers of petals open flat and quartered, and a ring of inner petals reflex around a green button eye. Colours are typically Gallica — cerise and purple, ageing through lavender and pale mauve, but softly blurred as if the dyes in some brilliant fabric had run in the rain.

On a more practical note, the bush is upright with greyish-green foliage and very few thorns.

Belle Isis (1845) Pale pink petals with a hint of peach open flat and beautifully layered, held within a ruffled cup. Flower have an unusual, delicious scent of myrrh and the bush is compact.

Camaieux (1830) Named because its form resembles a camellia, this rose must have created a sensation in Victorian England. The big ruffled blooms are boldly striped in white, cherry red, pink and mauve. Grow this and you can be trendy and nostalgic at the same time. (It's a bit too self-conscious to fall in love with though.)

Cardinal de Richelieu (1840) Crimson and purple ecclesiastical velvet, this rose reflexes into an exquisite, many-petalled ball of sheeny, slatey lilac-blue with a pale array of folded petals in the centre. Flowers are not large, but the richest of colours in this darkest of the Gallicas, aptly named for Cardinal de Richelieu, the power behind the throne of Louis XIII. The 'Cardinal' makes an excellent shrub but appreciates the luxuries of life more than some of its brethren. A little cosseting, such as good food and regular pruning, will keep this rose performing well.

Charles de Mills (Probably early 1800s, from the great French rose garden, Roseraie de l'Hay) This is a rich, dark, glowing jewel of a rose and each time I see it, I am astonished and enchanted anew. The blooms are huge without being blatant. They are flat, many-petalled, quilled and quartered, and the colours defy adequate description and are difficult to reproduce on film. The best I can suggest is wine, red and plum purple, paling to magenta and lilac, then slatey lavender before the petals fall.

Like the 'Cardinal', this is not a rose for candy-floss and marshmallow fans. (Or maybe it is, because it makes a wonderful foil for pastels — 'Belle Isis', for example.) The bush is of medium size, about 1.5 m, flowers profusely, and has few thorns. What more could one want? Well, perhaps a longer flowering period, as it blooms only in spring and early summer, but of course it will be there to delight us next year, and the year after.

'Complicata'

Complicata I can never quite work out why this outstanding shrub rose is classed as a Gallica, but leading rosarians have decided that it is. The flowers are simple singles and there doesn't seem to be anything in the least complicated about them, but no doubt the complications arise in tracing its lineage.

It grows to a handsome shrub — my three-year-old plant must be about 2 m high and 1.5 m wide. It is robust, reliable and free-flowering. The big single blooms are clear rose pink with pale centres and open wide to show golden stamens. In spring and early summer you couldn't find a prettier sight. Big orange hips are a bonus in autumn and it needs very little attention apart from the removal of dead wood. This is a rose that can cope with poor soil. I wouldn't be without it.

Duc de Guiche (1835) This is a magnificent rose with big fragrant blooms of wine-crimson apoplexing to choleric purple within a layered cup that opens to reveal a green eye. It is a moderate sprawly bush.

Duchesse d'Angoulême (c.1835) A rose with a delicate air, it is sometimes called The Wax Rose. Big cupped blooms open to a ruffle of blush pink, tissue paper transparent petals deepening to pale rose at the heart. Flowers are borne gracefully on an arching shrub with pale green leaves and few thorns.

Duchesse de Montebello (1829) Nothing could be prettier than the tallish, pear-shaped bush covered in spring and early summer with identical, perfectly formed, pale pink chiffon roses that might have decorated the neckline of a Victorian ballgown. This rose is one of my favourites.

Empress Josephine (early 19th century) (*R. francofurtana*) Parents thought to be *R. gallica* x *R. pendulina* Said to have been Josephine's favourite and mentioned by Redouté as growing wild in the hedges, the flowers of this rose are full-petalled, shallow bowls of deep pink petals with darker veining and lavender highlights. It has good foliage on a sprawling bush with very few thorns.

'Hippolyte'

Hippolyte (early 19th century) In colours this rose is not unlike 'Cardinal de Richelieu', with many-petalled, flat flowers reflexing into balls of cerise and violet which have pale highlights in the centre. Its long arching branches are covered all along with flowers which give it the most elegant habit of growth and it has very few thorns.

Ipsilanté (1821) Voluminous, quartered, lustrous lilac pink blooms open flat and softly crumpled. The bush is healthy and strong with good dark green foliage. This is a dear old rose with big beautiful fragrant flowers and deserves to be more widely grown.

Jenny Duval (18th century) A beautifully formed rose with typical heavenly Gallica fragrance and colouring, its mauves, pinks and violets are muted and softer, often deep rose in the heart, paling to iridescent mauve-pink on the outer petals. This is an upright shrub.

La Belle Sultane (*R. gallica violacea*) This is an ancient rose with big, slightly more than single flowers of deep crimson overlaid with violet and opening wide to show a ring of golden stamens. It has the look of a rich and rare wild rose. The bush is tall and strong and is one of the first Gallicas to flower.

Nestor (c.1840) Nestor is a beautiful rose which is cupped then opens flat and quartered, very like 'Belle de Crécy'. Its colour is magenta, paling to pink and mauve which is always deeper at the heart. A tall bush with good foliage, this rose has very few thorns.

Rose du Maître d'Ecole (1840) 'The Schoolmaster's Rose' is big, fragrant and full petalled, opening flat with fluted petals. Flowers are deep rose madder, veined with mauve and dusted with purple as the flower ages. Growth is lax, with canes arching under the weight of the heavy flowers.

Tricolore de Flandre (1846) Another striped rose with a theatrical flair, the name refers to three colours but most of the time I can detect only pale pink and blueberry splashed on the big, open double flowers. It is a low-growing, upright bush to about 1 m.

Tuscany (Old Velvet) (perhaps before 1500) As rich and romantic as the name suggests, this is thought to be the rose described in Sir Thomas Hanmer's *Garden*

Book: 'The Velvet rose, of a deepe murrey or purple colour, with some yellow thrums in the middle. The leaves are dark greene and spotted in some places with Red, somewhat larger than those of the common Red Rose. The prickles on the branches are very small and may be handled without offense.' The herbalist, Gerard, writing in 1597, also mentions a 'Velvet Rose' which seems to be the same variety.

'Tuscany's darkest crimson velvet petals surround a golden coronet of stamens. The flowers are sumptuous, scented and borne in upright clusters. On the practical side, it grows to an upright bush with good dark green foliage and few thorns.

Tuscany Superb (1848) This magnificent fragrant sport or seedling from Tuscany has superseded 'Old Velvet' and is the rose found most often in the nurseries today. The plant is slightly taller and more vigorous and the flowers have a few more petals.

'Tricolore de Flandre'

DAMASKS

Cleopatra, a lady well versed in matters aphrodisiac, is said to have instructed her servants to soak the sails of her ship in rose-water before she set off to meet Mark Anthony. It is easy to imagine those scented sails, pink tinged in the rays of the setting sun, wafting their fragrance on the soft Nile breezes, and underneath, the lady herself, trailing gauzy bits in the still blue water and idly scattering the perfumed pink petals of the Damask roses of the day.

Damasks are one of the most ancient, fragrant and romantic families of roses. Their antiquity is beyond doubt. On the island of Crete, a single form of the rose has been found painted on Minoan artifacts thought to be 4,000 years old. Dried garlands of roses that are clearly Damasks have been found in Egyptian tombs near the pyramids. The Roman Emperor, Nero, imported shiploads of Damasks from Egypt to strew on tables, floors and couches at imperial banquets, partly because it added to the ambience and partly because it was believed that the perfume cancelled the fumes of the wine and guests did not get drunk so quickly. (Bearing in mind the new-old science of aromatherapy, the idea may not be as silly as it sounds!)

In Jerusalem more than 1,000 years later, the Sultan, Saladin, used 500 camel-loads of Damask rose-water to purify the mosque at Omar after the expulsion of the Crusaders. It is thought that returning Crusaders brought the rose to England although, strangely, there seems to be no record of *R. damascena* in England or France until the 16th century. Henry VIII wore clothes that were padded with sachets of roses and lavender and we know that Elizabethan housewives used Damask and Gallica roses in the preparation of food, cosmetics and potpourris.

As to the name *R. damascena*, some say it refers to the city of Damascus where the rose was well known, but English rosarian and author Graham Thomas suggests that the name comes from a comparison between its petals and the delicate fabrics for which that city was renowned.

Most Damask roses are a deliciously perfumed blush to rose pink, frilly but refined, and a joy to have in the garden. They are usually taller than Gallicas, have light to greyish green leaves on pliable branches, stout, hooked thorns, and a little green ruff around the flowers. I have found them to be extremely hardy survivors, needing very little pruning apart from the removal of dead and spindly wood. You can cut them back if you wish, but be sure to do it at the right time, which is immediately after flowering for once-flowering roses, and near the end of winter for repeat bloomers.

As a general rule, Damasks flower in summer only. A notable exception is *R. damascena bifera*, which flowers right through to winter.

R. damascena bifera The Autumn Damask (Quatre Saisons) Thought to be R. gallica x R. moschata The flowers of this ancient rose are clear pink, richly perfumed, loosely cupped semi-double blooms with silky petals and have an unsophisticated charm. Blooms are often surrounded by such a cluster of buds that they have difficulty opening and end up in a muddled ruffle. When this rose was first established in France, it was sometimes called 'Bouquet Tout Fait', the 'Ready-made Bouquet', because the blooms and surrounding buds made a charming little posy. One of the pleasures of spring is to watch its new leaves emerge, big, crinkled, serrated, and the freshest clear pale green. The bush has a branching habit and usually grows from 1.5 to 2 m. As the name 'Quatre Saisons' ('Four Seasons') implies, this rose is capable of repeat flowering throughout the year and my bush certainly does.

'Ispahan'

Celsiana (pre-1750)   Introduced into France by the French plantsman Jacques Cels, this rose was painted by Redouté. Big semi-double, pale pink flowers emerge from sprays of dark buds, and layers of crumpled silk petals open wide to show a thick mop of golden stamens. The sprays of flowers and buds are surrounded by downy grey-green foliage on an excellent shrubby bush. This is a lovely rose to grow with deep blue perennials and silver foliage plants.

Ispahan (Pompon des Princes) (pre-1832)   An eminent rosarian and author of this century wrote that this rose 'stands erect with its flower whorls like a burning tree of roses with rose-flames for candles, and is not bowed down by them'. 'Ispahan's blooms are soft, warm unfading pink, full petalled and frilly, reflexing to pompoms with a button eye. The scent is glorious and it has a particularly long flowering period. A tall bush with plentiful, good foliage, give it room to arch its branches.

Kazanlik *R. damascena trigintipetala* (ancient)   This is one of the roses grown at Kazanlik, Bulgaria, for producing attar of roses for perfumes and cosmetics. It takes 3 tonnes of rose petals to make 1 kg of attar. Remember that when you wince at the price of good perfume! The rose itself is soft pink, loosely double and, of course, heavily scented. The bush is free-flowering, tall and lax.

La Ville de Bruxelles (1849)   The big, deep pink blooms are sumptuously curled, quartered and cupped, richly fragrant, and beautifully set amongst dark green leaves. The rose has a vigorous upright bush and should be more widely grown than it is.

Léda (The Painted Damask) (1827)   From fat, blunt buds that look as if they have been chewed by caterpillars bursts a frilly white skirt of a flower, each layered petal brushed with carmine on the edge, as if it had been touched with a paint brush. It is a pleasantly bushy plant with downy light green leaves.

'Léda'

Marie Louise (c.1813)   This is a very hardy old Damask often found surviving in abandoned gardens. Named for Napoleon's second wife, this sumptuous, glowing, many-petalled, deep pink rose with a tint of lilac opens flat with centre petals reflexing to show a button eye. 'Marie Louise' is a lax growing shrub with branches often weighed down by the weight of the flowers and is the perfect rose for potpourri.

Mme Hardy (1832)   This is a superb rose on which one can indulge that overworked word 'exquisite'. On smooth, almost thornless branches blooms a perfect-petalled, flat and quartered white rose with a little ring of petals folded inwards towards the centre around a jade green eye — 'white lace and emeralds', as I've heard 'Mme Hardy' described. It has heavenly Damask perfume, good foliage, and strong growth. (Monsieur

Hardy, Director of the Luxembourg Gardens in Paris, was the breeder, and 'Madame' his loveliest creation.)

Omar Khayyam (1893)   Grown from seed taken from the grave of the poet in Nashipur, this little lilac-pink rose is a bit like a raggedy starfish with a button eye. It is a small bush (about 1 m high), greyish green foliage, and it is prickly, but, with shades of the *Rubaiyat*, who could resist it?

ALBAS

While the flamboyant Gallica was associated with France, the Alba has long been associated with England. It is thought to have been brought by early Roman traders, but perhaps its white flowers flourished in the damp English dales and scented the misty mornings long before foreign ships touched the shores.

In ancient times, England was known as the Isle of Albion, and Roman historian, Pliny, writing on gardening at the end of the first century A.D., states that it might have been so named because of the white roses which abounded there. Certainly the Alba rose was one of the earliest to be cultivated in England and it is listed and illustrated in the 1597 edition of John Gerard's *Herball*. By then, presumably, Alba roses had been growing happily in monastery and cottage gardens for 500 years and more.

They were grown extensively in Italy, too. The white flowers in Botticelli's 'Birth of Venus' have been identified as Alba roses. They grew magnificently in Renaissance gardens and they grow magnificently in Italy today.

The original *R. alba* is thought to have been a natural hybrid between *R. damascena* (the Damask Rose) and a thornless, pure white form of *R. canina* (the Dog Rose).

Originally all Albas were white ('alba' is the Latin word for white), but gradually, soft pink hybrids were introduced without any loss of the delectable scent.

Even before you are captivated by the gentle beauty of an Alba rose, you will smell it: a scent rather like that of white hyacinths, but not as sweet — more complicated and elegant, reminiscent of the most expensive French perfume. Bushes tend to be tall, strong and exceptionally free of disease, perhaps because they conserve their energy for one glorious summer fling. They strike easily from cuttings and are capable of living to a great age.

Belle Amour   This was discovered by Miss Nancy Lindsay in 1950 in a French convent garden, but it is probably an ancient hybrid. Layers of soft salmon-pink petals frilled around deep amber stamens combine to make a rose worthy of its name. It is a strong shrub, growing to 2 m.

Celestial   Long, shell pink buds open to loosely double flowers with translucent petals of a soft, even pink. This is an ancient and very fragrant rose with an ethereal air. Flowers and buds are beautifully displayed amidst grey-green foliage on a tall bushy shrub with a graceful habit of growth.

Chloris (Rosée du Matin) (ancient)   A fragrant and almost thornless rose, 'Chloris' has powder pink blooms opening flat and layered to show an incurving knot of petals in the centre. A prolific spring and early summer flowering plus deep green leaves make this an excellent shrub rose.

Félicité Parmentier (1836)   Gently perfumed, pale powder-puff pink flowers packed with petals, beautifully formed and quartered, gradually opening flat, are borne in fragrant clusters on a well foliaged graceful bush. One of the loveliest of the Albas — and that's high praise indeed. Give it plenty of room.

Jeanne d'Arc (1818)   Very pretty, mud-

'Mme Legras de St Germain'

dled double flowers are cream with a tint of pink and fade to old ivory. Good fragrance and a medium-sized bushy shrub. This rose is named for the French martyr and saint.

Maiden's Blush (Cuisse de Nymphe; Incarnata; La Virginale; La Seduisante) (15th century) In France this delicious flesh pink rose is known by the seductive name of 'Cuisse de Nymph' (nymph's thigh) which probably describes the colour and texture perfectly. Victorian England could not cope with this bit of erotica and promptly christened it 'Maiden's Blush'. Whatever you call it, it looks and smells divine and is one of the delights of the Alba family. Flowers are loosely double and open flat with layers of soft petals, paling towards the outside. The plant grows to an arching shrub of about 2 m. There are two varieties of this rose available; 'Great Maiden's Blush' or 'Small Maiden's Blush', depending on the size of the flowers, not the maidens.

Maxima (Alba Maxima; Jacobite Rose; Great Double White; Cheshire Rose; Bonnie Prince Charlie's Rose) (15th century or earlier) A beautiful, big semi-wild rose of many names that has grown for centuries in the hedgerows and cottage gardens of the British Isles, 'Maxima's blooms are

large, very double, fragrant, and white with the faintest of blushes when young. It forms a very large shrub with plentiful, soft grey-green foliage. In Scotland legend has it that Flora MacDonald picked a white wild rose and gave it to Bonnie Prince Charlie who tucked it in his hat, and it became the emblem of the House of Stuart. Flowers only once but is an excellent hedging rose.

Mme Legras de St Germain (early 19th century) An aristocrat to her last exquisite petal and perhaps the most beautiful of the ivory-white roses, this rose is refined, frilly and generous with her blooms. The bush is tall — 2 m or more — and the fragrant flowers are borne all along graceful arching, thornless canes. This is a rose that appreciates a little dappled shade, although it does need sun for part of the day. I grow mine under tall tree ferns so that the long canes, heavy with flowers, can support themselves by arching up and over the ferny fans.

Mme Plantier (1835) This beautiful and distinctive rose is thought to be an

'Mme Plantier'

'Queen of Denmark'

Alba/Noisette hybrid, and it would be hard to think of a more fortunate marriage. Many-petalled and ivory-white with a ravishing jade green eye, 'Mme Plantier' has an airy habit of growth and slender thornless stems. Like 'Mme Legras de St Germain', it can be used as a tall shrub or a climber. I have seen it adding elegance and grace to a big purple rhododendron as it threaded its way through, or you could try it cascading from a tree. In Victorian times, this rose was a favourite for bridal bouquets and was often simply referred to as The Brides' Rose. It was also widely used as a memorial rose and can still be found in old cemeteries. The flowers are sweetly perfumed, leaves are fresh green, and it can cope with shade.

Queen of Denmark (Königin von Dänemark) (1826)   Recorded as a seedling of 'Maiden's Blush', roses don't come much more beautiful than this. From shallow cups, flowers open perfectly quartered, warm rose pink at the heart reflexing to a button eye, and framed by paler pink petals. Richly fragrant flowers grow on a strong bush with elegant, typically Alba, grey-green leaves.

Semi-plena (The White Rose of York) (pre 1600)   Identified before the 16th century, Semi-plena is thought to be the rose adopted as the emblem of the House of York during the Wars of the Roses. Flowers are semi single and the milk white petals open wide to show golden stamens. I love everything about this rose! The long, pink-tinged buds with their leafy sepals are the most beautiful buds in the world, the elegant simple blooms sit attractively in grey green foliage, and the scent is divine. It is summer flowering only, but a mass of bright hips is an autumn bonus and it makes an excellent hedging rose.

CENTIFOLIAS

This is another family of roses given a Latin name by Linnaeus. The name means 'a hundred leaves' and although the petal count of all Centifolias does not number precisely that, it is the sumptuous rose depicted by Dutch artists of the 17th century and later immortalised in Redouté's *Les Roses*.

For a long time it was thought to be an ancient species. Heroditus writing in the 5th century B.C. mentions a double rose 'having sixty petals and surpassing all others in fragrance', and other early writers have mentioned roses with a hundred petals. However, recent research suggests that the rose was the work of 17th century Dutch hybridists and is the result of a series of crosses using *R. gallica*, *R. moschata* (Musk), *R. damascena* and *R. alba*, with probably other species also involved. Whatever its lineage, it is a fantastic rose and perhaps the most fragrant of all.

It is sometimes called The Cabbage Rose because of its size and globular shape, but a brandy glass would be a more elegant comparison. I suppose you could compare the fat buds to little Brussels sprouts.

The heavy-petalled heads are inclined to hang, so it is a good idea to plant Centifolias in a raised part of the garden where you can look up to them and enjoy the intricately wrapped and perfumed heart of the rose. Shrubs are usually lax with arching branches and large leaves, often attractively wrinkled and serrated. Some of them colour well in autumn to compensate for departed blooms.

Remember that these once-flowering roses should be pruned (if you decide pruning is necessary) soon after flowering, and not in winter or you will cut away new season's flowers.

R. centifolia (Provence Rose, Rose des Peintres, The Cabbage Rose) (Cultivated prior to 1600) This is thought to be the

'Fantin-Latour'

old rose from which the group derived its name. Full, heavy scented blooms of a warm, glowing pink are borne on long stems. The bush is vigorous, with strong arching growth.
Blanchefleur (1835) Big, white full blooms revealing a tint of pink in the centre and heavily fragrant weigh down a thorny, arching shrub.
Fantin-Latour (c.1900) A mystery rose, perhaps not a true Centifolia, and named for Henri Fantin-Latour, the 19th-century French artist famous for his flower paintings. If you have ever flipped through a coffee table book of roses, you will have seen 'Fantin-Latour', one of the best known and most beautiful of all Centifolias. This is a ballerina of a rose: a hundred soft blush to mid-pink petals frill out in gently fluted layers to a big flat flower with an ethereal quality. To see it is to love it. What's more, the bush is free-flowering and vigorous, and will eventually

'Robert le Diable'

grow to about 2 m.

Juno (1832)   Named for the Queen of the Gods, this fragrant rose should be grown more often. Its perfumed double blooms are the palest pink and show a button eye when fully open. It forms an arching shrub to about 1.5 m and you can be sure of a profusion of flowers.

La Noblesse (1856)   Very big, scented double flowers of soft silvery pink are beautifully formed and open flat to a ruffle of petals. 'La Noblesse' blooms later than most Centifolias and its growth is more compact.

Petite de Hollande (Pompon des Dames) (c. 1800)   This is the Centifolia for small gardens. Pale pink flowers with a rosy heart are small, but retain their full-petalled charm. Borne in clusters, they are perfect for a bedside bouquet. The tidy bush grows to about 1 m.

Petite Lisette (1817)   This is another rose for the small garden with scented pompoms of deep rose pink.

Robert le Diable   The real Robert le Diable became Duke of Normandy in 1028, but the more recent introduction of his namesake is not recorded. A lurid cerise with overtones of purple, this rose opens a bloodshot green eye now and then. In my garden I find him not at all devilish, but a small shrub that might be interesting beside 'Petite de Hollande'.

The Bishop   A proud upright rose with a touch of Gallica and tough as old boots, 'The Bishop' blooms prolifically. Full-petalled in cerise purple with a silvery lilac reverse, clusters of flowers open to rosettes that pale to slatey purple as they age.

Tour de Malakoff (Black Jack) (1856)   This is a distinctive, big, bold, loosely formed magenta, purple and lavender rose. It is sometimes called The Taffeta Rose because the colours merge with age and weather and become almost iridescent like old watered silk or taffeta. It grows to a tall arching bush and can be trained upwards through shrubs that will support it, or its long flexible canes can be bent over and pegged down so that it throws out flowering shoots all along the branches.

'Tour de Malakoff'

Village Maid (La Rubanée) (1845) If you want a striped Centifolia, this is it. Big, blush-cream cupped blooms are striped in deep magenta-purple. The bush is vigorous and free-flowering. This is one of the roses often found surviving in old gardens. Its long sprays are ideal for flower arrangements.

MOSS ROSES

The sweet Moss rose conjures up Victorian England with all its sentimentality. Posies of scented Moss roses carried messages of love, were pinned to corseted bosoms and clasped in languid hands: and, no doubt, the individual blooms were pressed in many a maiden's tear-stained diary.

The blooms are very like those of the Centifolia. In fact, Moss roses began as a mutation from Centifolias. The buds, and sometimes the stalks and leaflets, are covered in 'moss'. It can be soft and downy or stiff and whiskery, and it is usually aromatic to the touch. Some roses have a lot, some have a little. Sepals around the buds are often prettily fringed and winged. All this charming packaging adds another dimension to the rose and it would be hard not to be enchanted by a pink Moss rose in its ferny bed.

If you plan to prune, check on the particular rose's flowering habits. Most flower only once and need to be pruned after flowering, but some are repeat bloomers and these can be pruned in winter.

***R. centifolia muscosa* (Common Moss Rose, Old Pink Moss) (pre 1700)** The oldest and one of the nicest Moss roses, this rose has warm pink, Centifolia-like blooms and intense fragrance. Lavish mossing on sepals and stalks releases an aromatic perfume when touched.

Alfred de Dalmas (Mousseline) (1855) A charming and delicately pretty blush pink,

'Chapeau de Napoléon'

semi-double flower opening to show deep golden stamens, its buds are well covered with soft green and russet moss and the foliage is lush. The bush does not grow to much more than 1 m and it repeat flowers throughout summer.

Capitaine John Ingram (1856) The rose was bred in France but the brave captain sounds decidedly English — I wish I knew who he was. Big plum-purple blooms have a silvery reverse to the petals and are heavily perfumed. There is not much moss though, and the bush is tall, lanky and thorny.

Chapeau de Napoléon (Cristata, Crested Moss) (1826) A fascinating rose, you might buy this one for the name alone. The fringed and mossy sepals project from the buds in such a way that they resemble little three-cornered hats like the French tricorne that Napoleon often wore. Full pink flowers paling to silvery mauve have that typical heavenly old-rose scent.

Comtesse de Murinais (1843) This exquisite, fragrant, faintly blushing white Moss rose set in bright, light green leaves is perfect for a bride's bouquet. Long, flared, mossed

'Eugénie Guinoisseau'

sepals enclose white buds sometimes tinged with pink. Full flowers open flat to reveal a button eye. The moss itself exhales an aromatic perfume when touched. It has luxuriant foliage on a bush that will reach 2 m and could need support.

Eugénie Guinoisseau (1864) Buds enclosed in green moss open to big fragrant cups of cerise, pink and deep violet petals. The bush is tall and upright and will repeat flower if well treated.

Général Kléber (1856) A loosely double rose with silky crumpled petals of clear pink, 'Général Kléber' has overtones of lilac and lots of fresh green moss on the buds. The bush is tall and healthy, the foliage is lush and there are very few thorns.

Gloire de Mousseux (1852) Big, soft, fragrant, many-petalled blooms of a clear unchanging pink are very beautiful and this

rose has the largest flower of all the Moss roses. Buds are mossed in green and the plant is bushy with light green leaves.

James Veitch (1865) Dusky crimson-purple flowers with a silver sheen on the backs of short petals open flat and reflex in the centre to a silvery button eye. An appealing dark rose with perfumed blooms and aromatic moss, 'James Veitch' will flower all summer. Just to balance things out, the bush is stout, prickly and prone to mildew.

Jeanne de Montfort (1851) Burgundy moss covers the long sepals of buds that open to big clusters of scented, frilly clear pink flowers revealing yellow stamens. This tall plant can be trained as a small climber.

Maréchal Davoust (1853) Sacheverell Sitwell compares the colour of this rose to 'cyclamen steeped in a syrup of mulberry juice and red wine', and I cannot better that, except to add that he was describing a mature flower tinged with purple. Opening flowers are deep mauve pink, but whatever the precise colouring of the thick layers of petals, the effect is superb. Buds are covered with dark moss and the bush flowers freely.

Marie de Blois (1852) Bright pink flowers are muddled, frilled and heavily perfumed. 'Marie' is generous with her blooms, well mossed, often recurrent, and altogether well worth growing.

Mme de la Roche-Lambert (1851) Crimson buds, darkly mossed, open to globular flowers filled with purple petals which have a dash of magenta. A medium-sized shrubby rose, 'Mme de la Roche-Lambert' can have a flowery fling in autumn if treated well.

Mme Louis Lévêque (1898) This is a sparse mossing but heavenly rose with full cupped blooms in a shade of pink that is just right: not too candy-floss, not too strident, just a soft, warm, clear pink. Petals have a silky chiffon texture and roll back in semicircles in cup-shaped blooms held proudly erect on an upright bush. I first saw this rose

'Mme Louis Lévêque'

in Australia, flowering its heart out, and fell in love with it on the spot. What's more, it repeats well in autumn.

Nuits de Young (Old Black) (1845)   This is the darkest of Moss roses, with smallish, fragrant double flowers of deepest burgundy velvet lit by golden stamens. A bush of twiggy growth and small deep green leaves, the buds are darkly mossed and the rich colour of the blooms combine to ensure that it does not go unnoticed among the marshmallow pinks.

Pélisson (1848)   A vigorous Moss rose that eventually grows to a big compact shrub and flowers generously, its beautifully formed rosettes are deep mauve pink at the heart with paler outer petals.

William Lobb (Old Velvet Moss) (1855)   I am madly, passionately and irrevocably in love with 'William Lobb', preferably when he's gone off a bit and turning mauve around the edges. This is a rich, sumptuous crimson-purple jewel of a rose, full-petalled blooms conveniently goblet shaped for plunging a nose in and sniffing. And when you do this, you'll see that he has a golden eye — a ring of yellow stamens. Poor old 'William' doesn't get a chance to hold his petals for long because they are rudely ripped away for the potpourri basket. Nothing in this world is perfect, and the bush is thorny, tall, and a bit ungainly, best used as a small climber or at the back of a border, where it can be supported by shrubs and scramble through them.

CHINAS

The Irish poet Thomas Moore was inspired by the sight of the China rose, 'Old Blush', blooming at Jenkinstown House, County Kilkenny, to write a poem about the 'last rose of summer'. China roses are capable of flowering from early spring through to winter.

When roses from China were brought to the Western world, they carried with them the gene that would endow future roses with the quality of *remontancy* — literally 'to mount again', i.e., the ability to repeat flower throughout the season. We know that roses have been cultivated in China for a very long time indeed. Confucius (551-479 B.C.) recorded that many roses had been planted in the Imperial Gardens in Peking, and roses are depicted in very early Chinese works of art.

For centuries China was a strange and exotic land, forbidden to foreigners. It was not until 1842 that the British were permitted to use certain Chinese ports and the island of Hong Kong for trading purposes. After that date, most of the early roses imported to England were hybrids from Chinese gardens, particularly from the 'Fa-Tee' ('Flowerland') nursery outside Canton, but before that time they had been collected by more adventurous methods.

As any gardener who travels with secateurs, damp paper and plastic bags in the glove box will know, planthunters are an intrepid and fearless band, not easily daunted. We know that rose seeds were collected in China and brought back to Europe many years before China officially opened her doors. Perhaps these early botanists were a little like fisherman in the tales they told. There are conflicting stories of who was responsible for the introduction of the first China roses to England. The generally accepted account is that a pink China rose, probably the rose we now know as 'Old Blush', arrived in England by way of the Netherlands in the 1780s. A short time later, a red form of the rose was found growing in Calcutta and brought to England by a captain of the East India Company.

The pink rose was christened Parson's Pink China, and the red rose, Slater's Crimson China. These two roses, together with pale pink Hume's Blush imported from the Fa-Tee nurseries in 1810 and the soft yellow Parks' Yellow, introduced in 1824, became known as the 'stud' roses, and are largely responsible for the ability to repeat flower found in later roses.

We still grow many of the early Chinas as well as their hybrids. They are usually hardy bushes with slender stems and an airy habit of growth. Except for a few later hybrids, flowers are not particularly showy, shapely or voluptuous, but they have an enduring charm and there are several I would not want to be without.

Anna Marie de Montraval (1880) (polyantha rose x Mme de Tartas)   This is a small twiggy bush that covers itself with perfect double tiny white roses, smelling of violets, and grows well in a container.

Comtesse du Cayla (1802)   A big brilliant semi-single with petals of flame and copper with a glint of gold, the loose nodding blooms light up the slender bush from spring to autumn. The rose is named for Zoe Talon, Comtesse du Cayla, wise and witty last mistress and confidante of Louis XVIII.

Grüss an Teplitz (1897)   The rose that converted me to red roses, I grow fonder of it every year. My plant was a gift and at the time I had no place in the garden for a red rose. It was planted hurriedly in poor soil and not much sun, around a corner by a kitchen window, but it bloomed and bloomed and I kept opening the window so the heavenly scent could waft inside. Clusters of quite large, informal double flowers are not bright red, but velvety crimson with blue overtones and a silvery sheen on the reverse of the petals. You will smell its perfume before you see it in the garden. It does get mildew towards autumn but carries on regardless, and you can always spray. A friend has planted it as a superb hedge against a white picket fence, but it is also effective as a moderate climber.

Hermosa (1840) Said to be the favourite rose of King George V, 'Hermosa's rose pink blooms are full and cupped with outer petals rolling back prettily. The plant is neat, sturdy and bushy, good for the front of a border or for massing in a bed. You can depend upon flowers all summer.

Irène Watts (1896) The blooms are cream flushed with peachy pink in a delicately beautiful, loosely double form, faintly quilled and fluted a little like the beautiful Centifolia, 'Fantin-Latour'. Add to this flowers that are fragrant and a bush which doesn't grow more than 1 m and you have another perfect free-flowering rose for a small garden, or any garden for that matter.

Louis XIV (1859) This has perfumed double flowers of darkest royal red with golden stamens on a compact bushy plant that repeat blooms through summer.

Mme Laurette Messimy (1887) Endearing loosely double floppy blooms of rose pink petals lit by a yellow glow at the base.

'Grüss an Teplitz'

'Old Blush'

The bush is tall for a China, but bushy, and flowers for a long time.

Mutabilis Tipo Idéale (Origin unknown — probably an old Chinese garden hybrid) Painted by Redouté, this is an astonishing rose with a charm all of its own. If you think a single old-fashioned rose would bore you, plant 'Mutabilis' and you will feel like the Queen in *Alice in Wonderland* who could believe six impossible things before breakfast. The yellow rose you saw in the morning might be a red one by teatime. The flowers open a soft honey colour, change to rosy buff and finally to crimson before the petals fall, although this particular sequence of colours cannot be depended upon absolutely — it might happen in reverse.

The bush is extremely hardy and has a pleasant airy habit of growth to about 2 m. Don't put it among your voluptuous beauties. It makes an excellent specimen shrub or a fantastic hedge, and it flowers from spring through to winter.

Old Blush (Introduced in 1789 but much older) Thought to be the old Parson's Pink China and 'the last rose of summer' of the song, this indispensable old rose is the first to bloom in spring and the last to give up in winter. 'Old Blush' bears clusters of graceful,

'Mutabilis'

informal, double dusty pink flowers with a silvery reverse to the petals. Some nurseries list a bush form which grows no more than 2 m, as well as a climbing sport. Others say that the bush will climb if planted against a sheltered wall. I grow mine as a climber where it frames a window very prettily and goes on to decorate a gable. It is not a sensational rose, but it is fragrant, charming and reliable, and I would not be without it.

Sophie's Perpetual (An old variety reintroduced and named by Sir Humphrey Brooke of Lime Kiln in 1960) Sprays of shapely, double cupped flowers vary from deep pink to silvery pink. An excellent shrub or small climber, the bush has very few thorns and, like most Chinas, blooms long and generously.

PORTLANDS

The first of this group of roses with a dash of Damask and a passing acquaintance with Gallicas appeared in England towards the end of the 18th century and was named in honour of the third Duchess of Portland, said to be an enthusiastic rose-lover of the time. It was initially thought that she brought the rose from Italy, but research has shown that the lady never left England. So there goes the romantic notion that the first Portland rose was plucked from the garden of a villa in Tuscany in a soft Italian twilight and clasped to a noble bosom, and here again is one of those mysteries which add to the fun of growing old roses.

In his recent book, *The Companion to Roses*, John Fisher writes: 'A more likely explanation is that the rose was indeed imported into England, crossed there and then sent to France . . . by the Lee and Kennedy nursery which supplied roses to Malmaison'. He goes on to say that Kennedy probably suggested to André Dupont,

'Comte de Chambord'

Josephine's gardener, that the rose be called Duchess of Portland, not because she was a rosarian, but because she was the wife of the Duke of Portland. Portland was twice Prime Minister of Britain and a close friend of William Pitt, who had the power to allow John Kennedy to transport roses to Malmaison without hindrance from the British Navy. Whether or not its origins owe more to commerce than romance, French hybridists were not slow to see the commercial possibilities in breeding from this sturdy compact rose with the ever-blooming habit.

In the early years of the 19th century, the Portland roses were a considerable group, but they lost popularity when the luscious Bourbons and Hybrid Perpetuals appeared on the scene. As it happens, they contributed in a large measure to the breeding of the Hybrid Perpetuals. Today only a handful remain, most of them tidy, upright compact bushes ideal for the small garden. Looking rather like shorter versions of Damasks, the bushes are thickly foliaged and blooms are often borne 'on the shoulder', which means they have short stems and nestle prettily into the foliage. A ruff of leaves below the fat buds is a distinguishing feature. And, of course, most of them are highly perfumed.

Comte de Chambord (1863) This is a rose that belongs on a hat. Bright pink buds open to full blown blooms with concentric rows of short petals surrounded by larger wavy petals, rich pink at the heart, paling to a softer lilac pink on the outer petals. Blooms are big, beautiful and very fragrant.

The rose began life as a lady. Bred by a New York rose-grower, Daniel Boll, it was named after his wife and known as 'Mme Boll'. However, he did not market the rose in the United States and it was sent to France where it was given the name of a French nobleman.

Jacques Cartier (1868)   Layer upon layer of pale pink petals, sometimes deeper in the centre, opening flat, softly quartered, then frilly, make this an endearing rose. A ring of petals in the centre reflex towards a button eye. The neat and rounded bush is covered with blooms that sit up straight and pretty in the lush green foliage. It looks superb with dark blue or purple perennials. Named for the valiant French navigator who explored

'Jacques Cartier'

'Rose de Rescht'

the Gulf of St Lawrence in Canada, this gently pretty rose is particularly tough and will survive bitter winter snows.

Rose de Rescht   This gem of a rose was discovered in Persia by eminent American rosarian, Miss Nancy Lindsay. Who could describe it better?

'Happened on it in an old Persian garden in ancient Rescht, tribute of the tea caravans plodding Persia-wards from China over the central Asian Steppes. It is a sturdy yard-high bush of lizard green, perpetually emblazoned with full camellia flowers of pigeon's-blood ruby, irised with royal purple, haloed with dragon sepals like the painted blooms on oriental faience.' It blooms from spring through autumn. A word of warning, though: this rose needs hard pruning to encourage continued prolific blooming.

Rose du Roi 'Lee's Crimson Perpetual' (1815) (possibly Duchess of Portland x _R. gallica officinalis_)   Big round buds open to rich royal crimson, fully double flowers mottled with purple and fragrant. The bush is not tall, but dense and compact, and flowers for a long time. The rose was raised in France by the Comte de Lelieur, superintendent of the royal gardens, and known as Rose de Lelieur. However, at the insistence of the Comtesse du Cayla, confidante of Louis XVIII in his old age, the rose was rechristened 'Rose du Roi' after his reinstatement on the throne. It is an important rose because it was used in the breeding of the first Hybrid Perpetual.

BOURBONS

The first Bourbon rose was discovered growing on the French Ile de Bourbon (now known as Reúnion), a small island east of Madagascar in the Indian Ocean. It was a natural hybrid between Parson's Pink China ('Old Blush') and 'The Autumn Damask' ('Quatre Saisons') which the farmers on the island planted closely together for hedging. These two roses had little in common except the all-important ability to flower perpetually, and this they bequeathed to their offspring.

In 1817, a French botanist, M. Emile Bréon, who had been sent to establish a botanical garden on the island, sent seeds of this new hybrid to M. Antoine Jacques, the head gardener of the Duke of Orléans (later to become King Louis Philippe) at the Chateau de Neuilly, where it was painted by Redouté. A second-generation rose was raised, and by 1825 the Bourbon rose had arrived in England.

Here was a rose that had it all: charm, style, vigour, and a heavenly old-worlde fragrance inherited from its Damask parent. What's more, it could keep on flowering all through summer and still produce an abundant flush of blooms in autumn.

For half a century in the early years of Queen Victoria's reign, the Bourbon was high fashion. If you like your roses lavish, try a few of these luscious roses. Many-petalled, fragrant, voluptuous, generous, versatile and easy enough to grow, they will enchant you forever. They come in bush and climbing forms and among them you will find the perfect rose for the particular spot you want to fill. Many have lax, sprawling growth habits and lend themselves to training on pillars and trellises, or pegging down in the old-fashioned way. (See Chapter 2, page 11.)

For continuity of flowers you do need to feed Bourbons well. I find that regular foliar feeding with liquid fish manure throughout summer ensures autumn blooms and helps to banish aphids and black spot.

Boule de Neige (1867) The prettiest carmine tinted buds open to glistening, white-petalled, perfectly formed blooms which slowly reflex to ruffled balls. Add to this a delicious fragrance and you have one of the most beautiful of white roses. Foliage is glossy, the bush is reasonably compact, and you get a generous flush of flowers in early summer and again in autumn.

Bourbon Queen (1834) This is a first generation hybrid from 'Old Blush'. Big cupped,

'Bourbon Queen'

'Honorine de Brabant'

many-petalled, deep pink flowers, flushed and veined with lilac, are frilly around the edges as they open wide and very fragrant. A gloriously rampant, hardy shrub-climber, weighed down with heavy flowers all along its arching canes in early summer, it sometimes repeats in autumn.

Commandant Beaurepaire (1874) Instead of the usual dark stripes and splashes on a pale background, this rose has petals of carmine pink, flecked and striped with pale pink, mauve and purple. A good upstanding rose, as befits its name, it makes a strong spreading shrub with dense growth. Long,

'Mme Ernst Calvat'

pointed, pale, almost chartreuse-green leaves set the rose off to perfection. It is summer flowering only.

Coupe d'Hébé (1840) Long sprays of richly scented, rose-pink goblets, with wavy edges to the petals, fade to lilac pink but remain deeper at the heart. An enchanting tall shrub or pillar rose, it has one long summer flowering only. If you prune this rose as soon as flowering has finished, it will make fresh new leafy growth and need no later pruning, except for the removal of spindly branches and dead wood.

Honorine de Brabant A sport from 'Commandant Beaurepaire', with the same lovely leaves inherited from the Musk rose, this is my favourite striped rose. The stripes are not blotched and blatant, but delicately traced in lilac pink and rose-madder on a blush pink cupped bloom. I like to grow this rose near 'Mme Isaac Pereire'. Honorine's stripes both highlight and cool the vivid colour of 'Mme Isaac'. A strong plant that grows to about 2 m, it makes a wide arching bush.

Kathleen Harrop (1919) This is a sport from 'Zéphirine Drouhin' in a much softer pink with a darker reverse to the petals. Like 'Zéphirine', it blooms for a long time and has no thorns, making it altogether a beautiful and desirable rose in a colour that is easier to place than the harsher pink of its parent. It grows to 3 m or more and can be a big bush, a climber, or pegged down.

La Reine Victoria (1872) Layer upon layer of lilac pink petals curve inwards to form satiny, scented brandy balloons. The bush is slender and willowy and makes a superb pillar rose for a small garden. 'The Queen' is beautiful and perpetual, but watch out for black spot.

Louise Odier (1851) One of the most dependable repeat-flowering Bourbons, 'Louise Odier's blooms are an unvarying rose pink and camellia-like in form, with each petal precisely in place. Add to this a rich fragrance, a queenly bearing, and a robust bush of moderate height, and you have perfection, I suppose.

Mme Ernst Calvat (1889)   A superb sport from 'Mme Isaac Pereire', this rose has the same huge, many-petalled, double form and the same heavenly perfume, but the colour is soft pink, slightly deeper in the centre. New growth is a lovely burnished bronze. If you find 'Mme Isaac' a bit overpowering, you will love 'Mme Ernst'. I use my plant as a small climber to about 3 m, but it can be pegged down very successfully, or why not grow the two roses together on an arch or trellis.

Mme Isaac Pereire (1881)   The ultimate 'hat rose', this is a voluptuous uncorseted Victorian beauty and one of the most fragrant of all roses — I defy anyone to deny its perfume! The enormous blooms are very double, quartered, and a glowing deep rose-madder — 'Mme' is definitely not for the 'marshmallows and candy-floss brigade'. Left as a big shrub, her growth habits are somewhat ungainly and she looks her best when trained as a pillar or trellis rose. Plant her near a door or a window so that you can enjoy the perfume.

Mme Lauriol de Barny (1868)   I love this rose. Blooms are silvery rose pink with lilac undertones and sometimes an iridescent mixture of these shades, like the watermarked sheen on taffeta. Big full-petalled flowers open flat and quartered to a perfect circle. There is nothing in the least untidy about this well-behaved Victorian charmer, and the fragrance is strong enough to perfume the air and waft through your garden. There is a suggestion of sweet sharpness to her perfume, like the bouquet of a particularly delectable wine. I grow my plant as a small climber on a tripod with strawberry coloured foxgloves and pale mauve flag irises. It needs good conditions to repeat in autumn, such as a midsummer feeding and adequate water.

'Mme Isaac Pereire'

'Mme Lauriol de Barny'

Mme Pierre Oger (1878)   A sport from 'La Reine Victoria' and sometimes called The Shell Rose because of her translucent pearly petals, 'Mme Oger's blooms are goblet-shaped, borne in clusters and packed with creamy porcelain fine petals in the centre and rosy blush petals on the outside. Sometimes the cream petals are tipped at the edges with pink; sometimes hot weather turns petals deep pink. Often they unfold like a waterlily and sometimes they speckle in the rain. You must take your chances — this rose is worth it, but it does need to be treated well. The bush shows its China parentage in its twiggy upright growth. It stays reasonably small and is an excellent Bourbon for the small garden or a large container.

Souvenir de la Malmaison (1843)   Often acclaimed as the most popular old-fashioned rose in the world. Big, powder pink, quartered, scented and devastatingly beautiful, it will always be my special favourite because it was my first old-fashioned rose. It comes in both a bush and climbing form: the climbing form is certainly more spectacular. The bush is quite low — about 1 m — and in my garden it's a sturdy plant, but be warned: it does not like to be pruned, and I'm told it does better on its own roots, i.e., grown from a cutting rather than bought from a nursery.

So perfect a rose must be allowed one fault. 'Souvenir de la Malmaison' is a bit like the girl with the curl in the middle of her forehead — 'when she's bad, she's horrid'. The buds are so packed with petals that they 'ball' in wet weather, or, more precisely, when the buds remain damp, they turn into soggy, limp brown lumps that have been variously compared to rotten onions and liver paté. Mostly this happens early in the season and autumn flowers are sheer perfection. It's a fault I can put up with, but if you live in a high rainfall area, more particularly where the humidity is high, it may be a problem.

'Souvenir de St Annes'

'Souvenir de la Malmaison' commemorates the Empress Josephine's garden at Malmaison, the estate outside Paris to which she retired. After her divorce from Napoleon, Josephine's rose collection became her greatest passion.

Souvenir de St Annes (1950)   A comparatively modern sport of 'Souvenir de la Malmaison', this rose has fewer petals which means it doesn't ball in the wet. Not as heart-stopping as its parent, but a refined, free-flowering, pale pink rose with a delicate air. The bush grows to about 1.5 m.

Variegata di Bologna (1909)   This is a dashing rose with large globular blooms opening quartered, definite stripes and splashes of purple crimson on a white background. Peter Beales says it reminds him of blackcurrant jam and semolina, but don't let that put you off! 'Variegata de Bologna' is a distinctive and beautiful rose in its way, and will grow to a big shrub or a moderate climber.

Zéphirine Drouhin (1868) Climber   What a wonderful name! Who was the ethereal Zéphirine, named for a soft breeze, I wonder? I have to say that 'Zéphirine's colour, a bright, unrelieved cerise, troubles me a bit, but here is a good example of a rose that remains highly popular because it is more than a pretty face. The blooms are semi-double, frilly and borne in great profusion all through summer on thornless stems, which makes this rose ideal for planting near doorways or paths. Primarily grown as a climber, this is a cheerful rose for a white wall. 'Zéphirine' can also be used with effect as a large and spectacular shrub at the back of a border, perhaps with dark blue and silver foliage plants to keep her company.

'Zéphirine Drouhin'

NOISETTES

If you like yellow climbing roses, you will love the Noisette family. Not, I hasten to add, that all Noisettes are yellow. They can be milk-white, old ivory, apricot mousse, or tea-washed pink, but a sheeny, silky, soft true yellow is their trademark colour.

The birth of these roses in the early 19th century has been described as 'the result of an illicit love affair between the true Musk Rose and a China rose under the soft romantic light of a Carolina moon' which is true enough but a bit too much even for me.

When Parson's Pink China (which we now grow as 'Old Blush') arrived in the USA, John Champney, a prosperous rice plantation owner of Charleston, South Carolina, crossed it with *R. moschata*, the old European Musk Rose.

The resulting hybrid, which had the cluster flowers, fragrance, and climbing habit of the Musk Rose plus the semi-double pink flowers of Parson's Pink China, was duly christened Champney's Pink Cluster.

John Champney was pleased with his rose and sent several cutting-grown plants to a New York nurseryman, William Prince. He also gave seedlings to a neighbour, Philippe Noisette, a Charleston florist, who made his own crosses and raised Blush Noisette, a smaller and fuller petalled rose than Champney's Pink Cluster. He sent seeds to his brother, Louis, a nurseryman in Paris who named the resultant plants 'Les Rosiers de Philippe Noisette'.

However, French breeders were not impressed until a fresh strain of the original Champney's Pink Cluster arrived from William Prince in New York. They crossed this rose with Parks' Yellow China and the result was the first of the yellow 'Noisettes'.

The first Noisetttes were vigorous plants with the ability to bear great clusters of flowers that retained the true sweet old-rose scent. The long-flowering ability of the Chinas had been combined with the climbing habit and perfume of the Musks.

The development and popularity of these new roses ran parallel with that of the Bourbons and Teas and added a new colour — yellow — to the predominant pinks and reds of the climbing roses of the day. Later in the century they were interbred with climbing Teas and some of their distinctive characteristics were lost, although some very lovely roses resulted.

Aimée Vibert (1828) A direct offspring of the original Champney's Pink Cluster, pink-tinged buds open to pure white ruffled flowers borne in big trailing sprays at the ends of branches. Gertrude Jekyll wrote that 'Aimée Vibert', with its long flexible branches, is the ideal rose to grow up a tree so that its blossoms can cascade down. She used a broom to loop it into place.

Alister Stella Gray 'Golden Rambler' (1894) This is an excellent rose to cover a gazebo or to use as a very large shrub. Clusters of very double pale gold blooms, deeper at the heart and fragrant, cover the plant and repeat well into autumn. The original 'Alister Stella Gray' was the son of the English rose breeder Alexander Gray, whose wife Stella died when Alister was born — hence the unusual middle name.

Bouquet d'Or (1872) A rich, full rose of coppery yellow, 'Bouquet d'Or' is a vigorous, healthy climber with dark green leaves and should be grown more often.

Céline Forestier (1842) This exquisite climbing rose begins with a magnificent spring flowering and repeats well into autumn. It would have to go on my list of top ten roses. I love the way its pointed buds, striped in cerise and ivory, open to big clotted cream and butter gold flowers, flat and quartered, with a sweet spicy perfume. Give it a warm wall and a little extra care, and you will be well rewarded.

Claire Jacquier (1888) Yolk-yellow buds open to pale gold, loosely double, fragrant flowers in clusters. A pretty rose although it does not reliably repeat-flower, it is a vigorous and healthy climber once it becomes established.

Cloth of Gold 'Chromatella' (1843) Fully double flowers are a warm buttery gold, and the stems are long and ideal for picking. This is the rose that caused a sensation at the Third National Rose Show held at Crystal Palace in London. Like most Noisettes, 'Cloth of Gold' prefers a warm spot and, given the right conditions, can reach very large proportions, fringing verandas or climbing trees. This does not mean it is not for a suburban garden. Like all climbers it can be easily kept within bounds by regular pruning. I would like to grow 'Cloth of Gold' with the violet-blue rambler, 'Veilchenblau', or perhaps with a clear blue clematis twining through it.

Crépuscule (1904) Masses of loose informal blooms open deep apricot — that last flick of reflected sun in the evening sky — and pale to a soft twilight glow as the petals age. A big sprawly shrub or a moderate climber with glossy disease-resistant foliage and very few thorns, the rose is perfectly named for 'Crépuscule' means 'twilight'. It is at its most spectacular in early summer when it is covered in blooms from top to bottom, but it repeat flowers and remains attractive through the season. Be daring and grow it with velvety maroon salpiglossis and purple irises at its feet.

Jaune Desprez (Desprez à Fleurs Jaune) (1835) An utterly exquisite old rose, it has fragrant double flowers of primrose yellow, shaded warm peach and pinky buff, which open flat and quartered. There are generous flowerings in spring and autumn on this climber, and some repeat flowers in between.

Lamarque (1830) Clusters of big, intensely fragrant ruffles of white petals with a hint

of lemon in the centre on a vigorous climber, this rose has healthy, pale green leaves and very few thorns. Writing in *Potpourri from a Surrey Garden*, a fascinating fund of advice on gardens, houses, children, etc., the well-known Victorian, Mrs Earle, categorically stated that 'no garden is perfect without Lamarque', and who would dare argue? It's a vigorous, long-flowering climber and a joy in any garden, but it does need a warm, sheltered situation.

Mme Alfred Carrière (1879) This is a dream of a rose with an ethereal quality that belies her toughness. 'Mme' needs to be looked up to, preferably with the sun behind her, so that you can appreciate her transparent rumpled organza skirt of milky petals with their faintest blush of pink and strong fragrance. A vigorous climber with few thorns that will scramble up trees and cope with a certain amount of shade, she may

'Crépuscule'

look a bit spindly for the first season. Give it time — it's worth it. This is such a beautiful, perfumed rose that it should be planted where you can enjoy it to the full. Spring and autumn flowerings are magnificent. The

'Mme Alfred Carrière'

admirable Gertrude Jekyll grew it in great flowery swags along wires between posts.

Maréchal Niel (1864)   A beautiful seedling from 'Cloth of Gold', 'Maréchal's pointed buds and big full, fragrant sunshiny flowers, coppery-green foliage and vigorous growth make this a superb climbing rose, but it must have a warm sheltered position to give of its best. It was named for Maréchal (Marshall) Niel, Secretary of War to Napoleon III.

Reve d'Or (1869)   Lovely, loosely double, fragrant nodding blooms are golden as the name suggests, paling with age, and sometimes with a hint of pink. A moderate well-behaved climber with plentiful dark green foliage, it is suitable for the smaller garden.

RUGOSAS

R. rugosa alba

I have an elderly neighbour, still living in the isolated family farmhouse, who showed me with pride her grandmother's 'Japanese Rose'. It was, of course, a Rugosa, an easily recognisable oriental family that doesn't look at all like the conventional rose.

Rugosa roses are prickly peasants, but the prickles don't matter because you will prune them only when they get too big and need cutting back — which won't bother them in the least. I have mentioned the prickles first because, apart from that, everything else is in their favour. Don't be put off by their sturdy plebeian appearance. Most of them have blooms as aristocratic and beautiful as any rose I know.

Rugosas in their wild state are natives of western Asia, Northern China and Japan, and were first introduced into Europe in 1784 by Carl Thunberg, a Swedish botanist. An English nursery imported two varieties, but because these prickly shrubs did not resemble the accepted idea of roses and the blooms would win no prizes on the show bench, they were largely ignored by the gardening elite for a hundred years or more.

From the last years of the 19th century through to the present day, the Rugosa rose has gained recognition for what it undoubtedly is: one of the most remarkable and rewarding of garden shrubs. It is certainly as hardy as any wilding. The foliage is especially thick and deeply veined (rugose), not at all like a conventional rose leaf, and is a rich dark green that turns butter yellow and russet red in autumn. It flourishes in poor soil, particularly sandy coastal areas where nothing much else will grow. Once it is established, lack of water does not deter it and it shrugs off hot summers, strong winds and bitter winters.

These are the roses that grow wild in great masses along the seashore of the northeast coast of America. They perfume the air for miles around until a gale blows in from the sea and strips their petals in a day. In England they soften the edges of bleak and busy motorways where they live on petrol pollution and assorted rubbish flung from cars.

No aphid in its right mind will attack them and, apart from a few over-gently bred hybrids, they are remarkably disease-resistant. However, the more the Rugosa characteristics are lost, the more susceptible the plant becomes to common rose diseases. Cautious hybridising has resulted in a variety of deliciously fragrant elegant singles and sumptuous doubles. They flower from spring to autumn and, as if that were not enough, most of the singles and a few of the doubles set a generous array of fat crabapple-sized, shiny red hips when the blooms have gone.

In Rugosas, then, we have sturdy undemanding shrubs that give us fragrant and beautiful flowers, colourful autumn foliage and decorative hips which, incidentally, are particularly rich in Vitamin C and make excellent rosehip jelly.

R. rugosa alba **(1870)**   This rose is thought to be a true species, not a hybrid, and it is superb in every way. From long, pointed, pink-tinged buds, the big hibiscus-like single flowers open immaculately white and delicate as tissue paper, with a bright coronet of golden stamens at their heart. It flowers all through summer and into autumn, when the foliage turns butter yellow and it bears great bunches of tomato shaped hips. The bush continues to flower, so that often white flowers and red hips mingle. You can depend upon a spreading shrub that will eventually reach about 2 m and is ideal for a single specimen or a hedge. Don't be tempted to dead-head or you'll ruin your chance of the magnificent hips.

Agnes (1922)   Very hardy yellow roses are few and far between. Bred in Canada, 'Agnes' can stand up to anything weather or environment can hand out, and what's more, she's an exquisitely beautiful fully double and fragrant amber-yellow rose, paling prettily with age. The plant very quickly grows to 2 or 3 m with good typical Rugosa foliage. Use it for a shrub, a pillar rose or a hedge.

Belle Poitevine (1894)   A big semi-double, rosy mauve-pink flower opens out flat from characteristic long buds. The foliage is dark green and lush on an upright bush. This is one of the double-flowered Rugosas that occasionally sets dark red hips.

Blanc Double de Coubert (1892)   Yes, I know it's a bit of a mouthful, but it is an exceptionally beautiful loosely double white rose, sometimes called The Muslin Rose because of the airy transparency of its petals. It's a true ice maiden, pure white and superbly scented, which is no more than you would expect of a hybrid that has the exquisite old Tea rose, 'Sombreuil', for one of its parents. It grows to a big wide shrub, sets bright hips occasionally, though not always, and makes a wonderful hedge.

Conrad Ferdinand Meyer (1899)   Beautiful Hybrid Tea type flowers of the softest silvery pink and heavily fragrant are borne freely on a tall upright shrub that can be

'Blanc Double de Coubert'

'Roseraie de l'Hay'

encouraged to climb. The bush is vigorous and very thorny, and it is advisable to prune hard if you want it to flower at eye level and form a shapely shrub. Unfortunately, it is susceptible to rust and you will need to spray.

Fru Dragmar Hastrup (1914) This is perhaps the loveliest of the low-growing Rugosas. It seldom reaches more than 1 m high and forms a spreading bush. Big single flowers are the purest of pinks with delicate deeper veining and amber stamens. It continues to flower while it sets enormous tomato-shaped hips that turn a glistening mulberry in autumn.

Hansa (1905) This excellent rose, which I use as a hedge, grows to about 1 m, flowers freely, and sets a few hips in autumn. Big blooms are deep magenta with an overlay of purple, loosely double, sometimes opening flat, and scent the air as you walk past.

Lady Curzon (1901) Enormous rose-pink, single and scented flowers like crumpled silk are simple and elegant and could be mistaken for a particularly beautiful wild rose. The very thorny bush is open, arching, and can grow very large indeed. This is a good plant for the shrubbery or wonderful for the wild garden. It has one long flowering only, which it does not repeat.

Magnifica (1916) This is a most appropriate name for this rose which bears big cyclamen pink, double flowers with shorter petals around the centre, prominent yellow stamens and a green eye. Bright hips and flowers are found at the same time on a rounded bush.

Max Graf (1919) A trailing hybrid, 'Max Graf' will form a low ground-covering thicket over a large area. Flowers are single and clear rose pink with yellow stamens, but they do not usually repeat bloom.

Mrs Anthony Waterer (1898) This is a big thorny bush, but with flowers and foliage more like one of its parents, the Hybrid Perpetual, 'General Jacqueminot', than a Rugosa. Perfumed, deep red double blooms are lovely in early summer, but you get only one prolific flowering and a few repeat blooms later.

Roseraie de l'Hay (1901) This is probably the best known Rugosa, named for the famous French rose garden. Long elegant buds open to a very large peony-like bloom of iridescent crimson-purple, which is not at all garish, just rich and rare, heavenly scented, and almost always in flower. The perfume is unusual. I've heard it compared to sugared almonds, but it reminds me of a slightly spicy eastern incense, a bit like the old clove-scented dianthus. The bush is handsome, with abundant foliage, and can grow to 2 m or more.

Scabrosa (1960) This is a comparatively modern Rugosa, but a particularly good one. Extremely large, bright cerise, single flowers; tomato-shaped hips; foliage that colours well in autumn; and upright growth make this a good rose for a dramatic easy-care hedge.

Souvenir de Philémon Cochet (1899) A sport of 'Blanc Double de Coubert', this is a deliciously perfumed, primarily white rose like its parent, but the flower is many petalled, flat and frilly with a lovely blush pink ruffle of petaloids in the centre. It has been compared to a double white hollyhock, and I think I like it even more than its parent.

HYBRID PERPETUALS

My father loved Hybrid Perpetuals and I, too, have a sneaking preference for these big flashy fragrant roses, the fashionable darlings of the 19th century.

In *Classic Roses* Peter Beales writes: 'As a result of a fusion between the Bourbons and, it would seem, any other parent that came along, a race of roses appeared which, following the initial confusion, became known as Hybrid Perpetuals.' I certainly can't think of a better way of putting it.

They were big exhibition-type roses, bred for showing and so popular in the 19th cen-

tury that new hybrids were produced at an astonishing rate until they numbered in the thousands. Some were disease prone or too tender to be grown in the open. Most have disappeared, but the best have survived. Two good examples of roses that were superstars of the 19th century and are still available but not often grown today are 'General Jacqueminot' and 'Frau Karl Druschk'. 'General Jack', a shapely perfumed red rose grown under glass for florists, became so popular in New York that it was claimed 'there is not a bosom in New York on which the General has not nestled'. Although it has been superceded by better red roses, it has often played a role in their ancestry. 'Frau Karl Druschki' ('Snow Queen') was for a long time regarded as the very best white rose available. A big queenly rose, pink in the bud, it opens pure white but, sadly, it has no perfume.

'Ferdinand Pichard'

Baroness Rothschild (1868) Enormous shallow cups are packed full of scented, silky, pale pink petals, deepening at the heart. The leaves grow right up to the flowers and surround them prettily. The bush is pleasantly compact and long flowering.

Baron Girod de L'Ain (1897) A lovely curiosity with a mix of China/Bourbon/Noisette ancestry, this is a rich dark red rose with petals tipped with frosted sugar on their frilly edges. The bush is strong, healthy and shrubby, with abundant large leaves.

Baronne Prévost (1842) Extremely large blooms of deep rose pink open flat and precisely ruffled within a frame of paler petals. This is a picture-book old-fashioned rose of great charm — and of course it smells divine — on a vigorous, well-foliaged bush.

Ferdinand Pichard (1921) This is a 20th-century Hybrid Perpetual and a truly flashy one. The Victorians would surely have approved of this big stylish striped concoction of pale pink and magenta-purple petals curling within a cup. Foliage is lush and the bush stays fairly small — the ideal rose to cut a dash in a small garden.

Mrs John Lang (1887)   A Victorian beauty, big, rose-pink and richly fragrant, profuse and recurrent, this is a rose I enjoy. I love the way her inner petals curl around her cabbagey heart while outer petals provide a frame, and it is obvious that the judges at rose shows did too. Bred in England by Henry Bennett, this rose was his greatest triumph and became so sought after that he was paid £45,000 for the distribution rights in America, an unheard of sum for a rose in those days.

Paul Neyron (1869)   Absolutely huge rich pink ruffled flowers with a paler reverse and a heavenly scent are hard to overlook. This show stopper was once seen in all the best places but seems to have fallen out of fashion. A little over-dressed for today perhaps, but it perfectly complemented plush Victoriana.

Paul Ricault (1845)   Full-petalled globular flowers of bright rose pink open flat and

'Reine des Violettes'

sometimes quartered with reflexing centre petals. This is a sumptuous rose on a vigorous upright bush.

Prince Camille de Rohan (1861)   Said to be the darkest of all roses, the 'Prince' lives up to his romantic name. Big, full, fragrant blooms of deep velvety red, darkly shadowed with maroon, weigh down the arching canes of a bush that does not grow more than 1 m. The 'Prince' has a weak neck so it is a good idea to plant him in a raised bed. Wouldn't you just know it, his constitution is a bit suspect too, but he does respond to tender loving care and he *is* handsome!

Reine des Violettes 'Queen of the Violets' (1860)   There is a touch of Gallica in this Hybrid Perpetual. Think of pastel crayons of pink, magenta, lilac and purple, smeared and smudged together, and you will have an idea of the colour of the petals. Add a pale highlight in the centre of the blooms which open flat and quartered. The bush is tall — about 2 m — with soft, grey-green leaves, hardy and thornless. A rose that always makes me think of Queen Victoria and that era of plum-purple plushness, 'Reine des Violettes' ranks high on my list of favourite roses. It is certainly my favourite Hybrid Perpetual.

Souvenir du Docteur Jamain (1865)   Another richly perfumed rose with beautiful form, its dusky wine-red blooms open to a velvet-petalled shallow cup and show golden stamens. Flowers are inclined to scorch in hot sun but are quite beautiful at their best. The bush is tall and angular.

Vick's Caprice (1891)   Found in the garden of Mr Vick of Rochester, New York, this sport from the pure pink 'Archiduchesse Elizabeth d'Austriche' has petals striped and flecked in pink and lilac. One of the more subtle combinations in striped roses, this is an entirely charming big, full-petalled rose with a delicate air. It sits upright, well surrounded by leaves on a bush with few thorns.

TEAS AND HYBRID TEAS

Early Tea roses were carried to Europe along-with cargos of tea by the tea clippers, ships of the East India Company. They were referred to as 'tea-scented roses' because they were said to smell like a newly opened chest of tea. Their perfumes are varied and delicious but none of them smell remotely like tea to me. To be fair, though, I've been told that they smell like crushed *fresh* tea leaves — and perhaps that's the faintly herbal and refreshing scent I detect in my *R. gigantea* hybrid, 'Lorraine Lee'.

In his book *Classic Roses*, Peter Beales describes their origins: 'These had, like their very close relations the Chinas, originated in the Orient and were probably the result of a much earlier programme of hybridising by the Chinese, or chance crosses between *R. gigantea* and *R. chinensis*. Like the Chinas, they had the desired characteristic of pro-longed flowering.

'The first to arrive in Europe was *R. indica odorata*, soon to become known as Hume's Blush after Sir Abraham Hume to whom it was sent from the Fa-Tee nurseries in Canton in 1810. The second came in 1824, found during an expedition to China to collect plants for the Royal Horticultural Society. This was later classified as *R. odorata ochroleuca*, but its original name of Parks' Yellow Tea-scented China, after its collector John Parks, has been used ever since'.

There were other early roses involved but to put it briefly and simply, Tea roses were bred from pink and yellow Chinese roses and have inherited the long flowering habit and subtle colours of their ancestors. The Victorians loved them and grew many of them in conservatories because they were not considered hardy enough for the English climate, although the buds were perfect for gentlemen's buttonholes.

In the main, Teas resent hard pruning. It

'Dainty Bess'

pays to remove dead and spindly wood and prune only lightly, but deadhead conscientiously.

Hybrid Teas evolved from crossing Teas with Hybrid Perpetuals and were really the result of the hybridisers attempts to satisfy the public's demands for novelty. From a flurry of hybridisation there emerged some very lovely roses but a certain degree of confusion when it came to their classification. However, what concerns us here are the roses themselves. We still grow a fair number of the old Hybrid Teas, although I have space to list just a few. The roses mentioned here are primarily bush roses. A separate chapter is devoted to Climbing Hybrid Teas. Of course many modern roses come into this group.

Anna Pavlova (1981) Hybrid Tea Although a comparatively recent introduction from the nursery of English rosarian and author, Peter Beales, 'Anna Pavlova' cannot be left out of the old-rose garden. The softest of pink flowers are large, full petalled and cupped. The perfume is superb and intense, reminiscent of the modern rose 'Fragrant Cloud'. Habit of growth is upright and tall and, in my experience, it resents pruning in its first year. This is a truly delicious rose.

Baronne Henriette de Snoy (1897) Tea Petals of creamy pink with a deeper reverse, and veined in carmine open to shapely fragrant high-centred double blooms on long stems, good for picking. The bush is tall, vigorous and free-flowering.

Bon Silene (Before 1839) Tea This is a very old, highly scented Tea with long pointed buds which open to rich rose-madder double blooms. Expect a profusion of flowers on a compact plant.

Catherine Mermet (1869) Tea One of those elegant old Teas that bloom forever, 'Catherine' has rosy-tipped pale pink buds opening to big double lilac pink flowers on long stems perfect for picking. I've heard them described as 'scented stiffened silk', but it hates rain.

Dainty Bess (1925) Hybrid Tea An offspring of the great 'Ophelia', this is a superb rose. Gone is the overstuffed opulence of Victoriana. We're looking at the 1920s here with chemise dresses, short skirts and tea dances. If you think you don't like single roses, 'Dainty Bess' will change your mind. Clusters of long slim buds open to silvery pink wavy-petalled blooms with golden brown stamens. 'Dainty Bess' flowers prolifically and repeats. There is a moderate bush and also a climbing form which is ideal for a pillar. Like many single roses, 'Dainty Bess' dies well. Petals fall and only the lovely stamens remain.

Duchesse de Brabant (1857) Tea This is one of the most graceful, free-flowering Teas. Pearly pink, cupped and fully double flowers are borne in profusion. Flowering occurs early and continues until winter. Foliage is fresh apple green, healthy and plentiful. The vigorous bush is more shrubby and well foliated than most, and can grow to 2 m, given time.

Ellen Willmott (1936) Hybrid Tea What do you get when you cross 'Dainty Bess' with 'Lady Hillingdon'? If you are exceptionally lucky, you get a superb big single rose with wavy petals of pink and cream and long golden stamens, offset by dark green foliage on a strong upright bush: good enough to name after the famous English rosarian.

General Gallieni (1899) Hybrid Tea A remarkable rose of great distinction, fittingly named for the French general who was responsible for the defence of Paris at the beginning of World War I. As the bud opens, it seems that a tight posy of buff yellow rosebuds has been crammed into a cup of carmine petals, but once the unruly petals unfold and begin to fling themselves about, anything can happen. No two roses seem to be precisely the same and to complicate things further, the big double flowers change colour with the seasons. The 'General' blooms from spring through autumn when the blooms darken to a sombre chestnut red. It is a tall, strong, hardy bush with few thorns.

Grace Darling (1884) Hybrid Tea I have a childhood memory of a picture of Grace Darling, daughter of the lighthouse keeper, rowing bravely out through ferocious seas to rescue the shipwrecked sailors. I planted this rose for no better reason than that it was named for the young Victorian heroine. I was not disappointed. It's a full-petalled rose, opening flattish, a true clear pink, shading to creamy-white on the outer petals. 'Grace' is very pretty and not very big, growing to about 1 m.

Jean Ducher (c.1900) Tea Sometimes I think this is my favourite rose of all. The flowers are distinctive. I know of no other rose with petals arranged in quite the same

'Grace Darling'

'Jean Ducher'

way, like layers of loosely folded silk. The blooms are large, peaches-and-cream pink, and sweetly fragrant. The bush is well shaped and almost thornless with wine-red new wood, but perhaps the most endearing virtue is that it bursts into bloom in early spring and continues well into winter. It is mid-winter and snowing as I write and if I look out the window, I can see there are still buds on my 'Jean Ducher'. Nothing in life is perfect though, and a friend did comment that 'Jean' has ugly legs. Blinded by the beauty of the flowers, I hadn't noticed, but perhaps he does need a froth of something — nigella or gypsophila perhaps — to hide his knobbly knees.

La France (1867) Hybrid Tea This is an important rose because it is considered to be the first Hybrid Tea, the result of crossing a Tea rose and a Hybrid Perpetual. An instantly recognisable and elegant silvery pink, high-centred double with outer petals that

roll back to points, long graceful stems, and a deceptively light and delicate air, 'La France' blooms profusely for most of the summer. It is a hardy bush which can reach at least 1.5 m or more and withstand harsh winters.

Mrs Oakley Fisher (1921) Hybrid Tea Clusters of big mandarin yellow single flowers with amber stamens are highly scented — and a sheer delight. It is an upright bushy plant.

Ophelia (1912) Hybrid Tea A popular rose throughout the 20th century and probably beyond, beautiful buds open to superbly shaped, high-centred fragrant blooms of flesh pink, darkening in the centre and lit by a touch of yellow at the base. 'Ophelia' is an upright bush of moderate size. A climbing sport of this rose was introduced in 1920.

Peace (1945) Hybrid Tea At 50-plus not quite an old rose but, like others I have chosen to include, this classic is too important to omit. A big beautiful scented fruit-salad of a

'Peace'

rose on a strong bush, colours vary with the season but are primarily pale yellow, lightly suffused with pale pink and cerise. Vita Sackville-West hated it and thought it vulgar — and it took me a while to learn to appreciate it — but a bowl of 'Peace' roses are hard to resist. A climbing form was introduced in 1950.

Rosette Delizy (1922) Hybrid Tea The delightfully named 'Rosette Delizy' has 'General Gallieni' for a parent and inherits the same colouring but in a less haphazard fashion. Centres of yellow ochre shading to apricot are surrounded by outer petals of deep coppery rose. Flowers are fragrant and foliage is bright shiny green, healthy and plentiful. Rosette is a generous and prolific bloomer, and a moderate bush suitable for a small garden.

Shot Silk (1924) Hybrid Tea If you tire of the pastel pinks, try this perpetual bloomer with the classic Hybrid Tea form and silky petals that are a mix of rich rose-madder and salmon, shading to lemon gold in the centre. A rose that was planted in everyone's garden 40 years ago, 'Shot Silk' seems to have dropped out of favour which is a pity because it is not only beautiful but one of the hardiest and most forgiving of roses. It is available in bush and climbing forms.

CLIMBING TEAS AND HYBRID TEAS

Allen Chandler (1923) Hybrid Tea Old red roses are not thick on the ground or in the trees and therefore I cannot resist including one or two of moderate age. Just two layers of bright red velvet petals around a ring of golden stamens make this a superb and elegant rose, not too lush and overpowering. 'Allen Chandler' is a hardy climber with good dark green foliage and a long flowering habit which you will enjoy. It pays to deadhead as much as possible for continuity of blooms.

Cupid (1915) Hybrid Tea Big single flowers with wavy petals of peachy pink, paling at the heart to emphasise amber stamens, make this rose one of the most bewitching of climbers. It is summer flowering only, but grow it over an arch with the ever-blooming, porcelain pretty 'Phyllis Bide' (see page 87) or a late summer-flowering clematis.

Devoniensis 'The Magnolia Rose' (1858) Tea Big blooms, pink-tinted in the bud, open flat and quartered, the colour of clotted Devonshire cream with the velvety texture of magnolia blossoms. An early Tea and one of the nicest, the bush form was introduced in 1838 and the more popular climbing form appeared 20 years later, bred in Devon, where else? Few thorns, splendid reddish green foliage and wine-red new growth add to its considerable charms.

Fortune's Double Yellow (Beauty of Glazenwood, Gold of Ophir) (1845) Tea Discovered in a mandarin's garden in North China by celebrated plant hunter, Robert Fortune, this has loosely double, fly-away flowers of coppery flame and honey buff. A big bush in full bloom will stay in your mind's eye forever. It needs a warm sheltered position to give of its best, takes a while to get established, and has only one long fantastic flowering, beginning in early summer, but it is definitely worth growing. A shrub climber with very few thorns, it can

'Lady Hillingdon'

grow to a great height, given time, and is better left unpruned, although a tidy-up immediately after flowering is permissible.

Gloire de Dijon (1853) Tea   This is a much-loved rose with big, full, fragrant flowers opening flat with silky, crumpled and quartered petals. Colours can vary from warm coppery buff to pale gold. Author H E Bates goes further and compares them to 'a creamy elegant bosom, slightly flushed'. I don't know how the Reverend Dean Hole would have felt about that — it was his favourite rose. Flowering begins early in the season; there are some repeat blooms, and often a good flush in autumn.

Guinée (1938) Hybrid Tea   A fully double rose with heavy velvet petals of darkest unfading crimson and an intoxicating fragrance, 'Guinée' is all that a romantic red rose should be. You will get a generous flowering early, then repeat blooms, and sometimes a bonus in autumn.

Lady Hillingdon (1917) Tea   This is an elegant Tea with pointed apricot buds that open to nodding buff-apricot, semi-double flowers displayed to perfection by bronze stems and plum-coloured new foliage. An early flowering climber with a fresh Tea fragrance, 'Lady Hillingdon' will repeat bloom through to autumn in a warm sheltered spot.

Lady Waterlow (1903) Hybrid Tea   An absolute charmer, 'Lady Waterlow' has big, loose, scented, semi-double blooms and petals that are peachy pink, often veined and edged in a darker shade. This is an easily managed climber that flowers for a long time — plant it to cover a pillar or trellis.

Meg (1954) Hybrid Tea   Not yet 50 years old but too good to exclude, 'Meg's big single flowers are devastatingly beautiful. Petals flushed apricot, peachy pink and buff yellow flare out from a distinct ring of russet stamens. Foliage is dark and glossy and canes are inclined to be stiff and upright rather than pliable, so that 'Meg' is at her best with the support of a wall. She repeat blooms throughout summer if you deadhead.

Mme Caroline Testout (1901) Hybrid Tea   Deep silvery pink blooms are large, lush, and cabbagey with rolled petals and a strong sweet fragrance. This rose was bred in 1890

'Mme Caroline Testout'

by the brilliant French hybridist, Joseph Pernet-Ducher, who reportedly didn't think much of it as a seedling, but along came Mme Testout, a Parisian dress-designer with an eye for a good advertising gimmick. She bought it, named it after herself, and it was launched in her London showroom in the spring of 1890. This was a shrewd move because, with the right promotion, the rose became highly popular and her salons prospered, always decorated lavishly with her own lovely roses.

A vigorous climbing sport was introduced in 1901 and this is the rose we grow today. A profuse and recurrent bloomer with good foliage, it covers walls and pergolas beautifully.

'Souvenir d'un Ami'

Mme Grégoire Staechelin (Spanish Beauty) (1927) Hybrid Tea Bred in Spain, this is a soft and gracious double rose with delightfully wavy petals of dusty pink, deepening in the heart, and a strong sweet-pea fragrance. It is a vigorous climber that blooms early and freely, but only once. If you don't deadhead, you get a bonus of mammoth and magnificent hips in autumn, perhaps the biggest hips of any rose. She looks wonderful combined with wisteria and blooms at about the same time. You can prune them both after flowering, but you will miss 'Mme Grégoire's hips.

Mme Jules Graveraux (1901) Tea This is a shapely double rose with rolled and sometimes quartered petals of buff-yellow with peachy-pink undertones. A sweet perfume and lush healthy foliage make for a good all-rounder, and the flowers look lovely in a vase too. It was named for the wife of Jules Gravereaux, director of the famous Roseraie de l'Hay and author of *Les Roses*, published in 1912.

Paul's Lemon Pillar (1915) Hybrid Tea Extravagantly large and queenly double roses of palest lemon mousse and cream are fragrant and perfectly complemented by big dark leaves. This is a free-flowering robust climber.

Safrano (1839) Tea One of the oldest Teas and a lovely example of a rose that shows the yellow colouring of its China heritage, 'Safrano's beautiful long, pointed, saffron yellow buds were once seen in all the best florists' windows. Semi-double flowers are peachy buff with a yellow base and graced many a garden when yellow Tea roses were the last word in elegance. 'Safrano' will grow vigorously and flower from spring to autumn, but it does appreciate warmth and shelter, so choose its position carefully.

Sombreuil (1850) Tea Exquisite ivory white blooms open flat, quartered and richly scented. 'Sombreuil' is a much-loved old rose that repeat flowers, has lush green foliage, and does not grow too big. For a sheltered spot and a little care, you will be well rewarded.

Souvenir de Mme Léonie Viennot (1897) Tea This is a deliciously fragrant double in a warm sun-kissed blend of coppery pink and primrose. It makes a big shrubby climber and is capable of flowering through to winter in a temperate climate. Be judicious in your pruning because this rose flowers on old wood. It is probably better left unpruned except for the removal of dead wood.

Souvenir d'un Ami (1846) Tea A healthy moderate climber with few thorns, 'Souvenir d'un Ami' can repeat all summer and still produce a magnificent display in autumn. Its big double fragrant flowers are deep rose pink, shaded with salmon and primrose.

HYBRID MUSKS

The Reverend Joseph Pemberton is credited with the introduction of a group of roses, some large, some small, but all exceptionally beautiful, disease-resistant and long-flowering, which were eventually christened the Hybrid Musks, although their connection with the Musk rose is marginal.

Roses and the country clergy seem to have had a certain affinity for each other, or perhaps these rural gentlemen, having dealt with the Sunday sermon, had time on their hands for the purest of pleasures. The first president of Britain's National Rose Society was Samuel Reynolds Hole, Dean of Rochester, an ecclesiastical gentleman with a vast practical knowledge of roses. In 1869 he published *A Book About Roses* which became a best-seller, went into many reprints and is often quoted today.

In 1894, the Reverend A Foster-Melliar of Sproughton Rectory near Ipswich, wrote *The Book of the Rose*, also a bestseller, and a few years later in 1908, the Reverend Joseph Pemberton published the all-encompassing *Roses; Their History, Development and Cultivation*. However, it is as a breeder of Hybrid Musk roses rather than as an author that he is remembered.

As a foundation for his breeding programme, the Reverend Pemberton used a French and a German rose, 'Aglaia' and 'Trier', which had *R. multiflora*, *R. moschata*

'Ballerina'

and a Noisette rose in their immediate ancestry. Hybrid Musks are a diverse group, but many of them retain the silky petals and soft colouring of their Noisette heritage, the robust growth of *R. multiflora* and the warm sweet scent of the Musk rose.

When Joseph Pemberton died in 1925, his sister, Florence, carried on his hybridising work for a short time, and then the entire collection of roses was handed over to the Pembertons' gardeners, John and Ann Bentall, who set up in business and subsequently introduced more Hybrid Musks. Most of these roses were released in the 1920s and 30s, so perhaps they are not quite 'old roses' yet, but because of their form, fragrance, and bushy habit of growth, they can usually be found in the gardens of old-rose enthusiasts.

Hybrid Musks are wonderful roses for the beginner, uniformly robust and not given to displays of temperament. You really can't go wrong. They will reward you generously and you will be hooked on roses forever.

Autumn Delight (1933)   And it is just that. Big clusters of amber buds open to fragrant semi-double, old ivory flowers with bronzy-red stamens that are exactly right in the garden when the heady opulence of summer has passed. The bushy shrub grows to over 1 m, has few thorns and the flowers last a long time on the bush — or in a vase.

Ballerina (1937)   Ann Bentall discovered this rose as a chance seedling, although the story goes that her husband never thought much of it. Ann persisted and 'Ballerina' was introduced to become an immediate and lasting success.

From a late start in spring, 'Ballerina' bursts into blossoms that last until late autumn. Individual flowers are single, small and dainty, deep pink at edge of the petals shading to white at the centre, and borne in truly enormous sprays. The rose is most often grown as a spreading shrub and forms a compact mound with branches arching to the ground. However, I have seen it used as a climber and trained up the grey stone wall of a house to reach about 3 m and frame a window very prettily. It is also ideal for bridging a gap between other roses in a border, but most of all I like to see it planted near water.

Bloomfield Dainty (1924)   This is a charming yellow rose bred in the United States. Long, pointed, bright apricot buds open to soft, yellow, single blooms, sometimes fading to creamy pink. The bush is upright and vigorous, and the foliage dense and glossy.

Buff Beauty (1939)   This is my favourite Hybrid Musk — all apricots and cream in spring and again in autumn. In a dry autumn, I've noticed some blooms can be blush pink.

'Buff Beauty'

American rosarian, Miss Nancy Lindsay, wrote 'Golden as a tiger, candied as a ripe apricot, gloriously spicy [to which I would add, "buff as a biscuit"] Buff Beauty holds my heart'. Deep apricot buds open to full-petalled, frilly, pale apricot blooms that fade to pearly buff. 'Buff Beauty' grows to a big well foliated bush that does better with support — I use a rustic tripod — or it can be used effectively as a climber. This is a rose that needs to be looked up to because its clusters hang down with the weight of the blooms.

Clytemnestra (1915)   A different and interesting rose by the Reverend Pemberton, 'Clytemnestra' has tight little buds of copper and gold opening to a big ruffle of muddled, jagged petals of softest salmon beige. Flowers are quite large, borne in clusters all along pliable canes. The bush is sprawly, vigorous and free-flowering. Peter Beales recommends growing this rose en masse for maximum effect.

It's a rose that makes me smile, partly because I like it and partly because I don't know what possessed a scholarly vicar who frequently dipped into Greek mythology for the names of his roses, to commemorate a woman who was definitely not a role model for the girls in Sunday School. However, Clytemnestra's life was tragic, and perhaps there is a hint of jangled nerves in the unruly pointed petals.

Cornelia (1925) This prettiest of roses, with layers of little coral-pink petticoats pinned with a golden brooch, has not just one flower but great luscious clusters of them. The fragrance is something special and has been compared to a mixture of heliotrope and narcissus, which sounds a bit nauseatingly heady but is, in fact, simply soft and sweet. Classed as a shrub-climber, 'Cornelia' can be trained easily over an arch or against a supporting structure. For a dramatic colour effect, plant it near *Cotinus coggyria*, the European smoke bush.

Danae (1913) Clusters of butter yellow buds open paler, then fade to a creamy buff with a touch of yellow in the centre. This is an appealing semi-double rose that sits nicely in a background of very dark green leaves. It repeats well through summer until late autumn when a crop of small orange hips replace the flowers. The bush is graceful and arching and can be trained to climb a little.

Francesca (1928) If you love yellow roses, try this one. Big sprays of yolk yellow to pale primrose, loosely double flowers, are beautifully framed by glossy green leaves. It is a vigorous upright bush, though not as big as that of 'Buff Beauty'.

Moonlight (1913) One of the first of the Hybrid Musks Pemberton bred from the German stud rose, 'Trier', 'Moonlight' is well named. Clusters of small semi-double flowers are ivory white, sometimes tinged with lemon, and richly fragrant. Viewed in the evening against dark wood and dense dark green foliage, they do have a luminous quality. I have seen this rose looking delightful planted as a hedge against a high brick wall. The bush is tall and flexible enough to train around pillars or along rope swags, or to be enjoyed for its quiet beauty as a loose, cascading shrub.

Penelope (1924) A seedling of the famous 'Ophelia', this rose is a sheer delight. A big sprawling shrub covered with fragrant semi-double flowers of mother-of-pearl and shell

'Penelope'

pink, with petals that frill at the edges, 'Penelope' is instantly recognisable in the garden. There is never the slightest possibility of confusing her with any other rose. Her endearing ways are continued in her habit of growth which is graceful and spreading with good dense foliage, plum red stems and few thorns. 'Penelope' will grow happily as a specimen shrub, in a mixed border, or can be used to make a splendid hedge.

Prosperity (1919) If I had my way I would replace our five million 'Iceberg' Floribundas (good rose though it is) with 'Prosperity'. It isn't as icy white but neither does it mark in the rain, and what's more, it's fragrant. Beautifully formed double, ivory-white flowers with the faintest reflection of a blush in the centres, weigh down the arching branches of a strong bushy shrub.

Sadlers Wells (1983) I'm including this modern Hybrid Musk, bred from 'Penelope', because it is spectacular. Big semi-double flowers, resembling 'Penelope' in form, are silvery pink, laced with cherry red, especially at the edges. 'Sadlers Wells' flowers all summer and will light up your garden in autumn.

Trier (1904) Bred by Peter Lambert of Germany and named after his birthplace, 'Trier' is an historic rose, the ancestor of the Hybrid Musk family which the Reverend Pemberton extended so successfully. Big clusters of small simple, cupped flowers are creamy white with a faint touch of pink. It is a dense shrub with tiny red hips in autumn.

Vanity (1920) A cheerful, showy, healthy rose, 'Vanity' has sprays of big wide-open, vivid cerise, semi-double flowers on long stems that are so fragrant they can perfume a room when picked. The bush is large, open and angular. It needs plenty of space and is good as a background shrub or it can be trained as a moderate climber.

Wilhelm (Skyrocket) (1944) Red Hybrid Musks are rare. This excellent comparatively modern rose was developed in Germany by Kordes. Clusters of big bright cherry red, semi-double, wavy-petalled flowers with a distinct yellow centre cover a healthy shrub that blooms forever. Good hips form in autumn/winter if you don't deadhead.

'Wilhelm'

SHRUB ROSES

Most old roses can be treated as garden shrubs. They are not meant to be pruned to a few sticks in winter, but they may need training and shaping to achieve the effect you want. Old dead wood and spindly growth should always be removed. The roses listed below are a mixed bunch, some low-growing, some tall, but they can all be grown as shrubs. Most look their best in a border with other plants, but a few, notably 'Fritz Nobis', 'Raubritter' and 'Stanwell Perpetual', have a sprawly habit of growth and great presence, and can stand alone.

Although many of the roses mentioned here are comparatively modern, they merit inclusion in the old-fashioned rose garden either because of their form or their habit of growth. Four excellent Pimpinellifolia hybrid roses bred by the Kordes nursery in Germany — 'Frühlingsanfang', 'Frühlingsduft', 'Frühlingsgold' and 'Frühlingsmorgen' — are also included in this section. Pimpenellifolia roses, which (just to confuse us) used to be called Spinosissimas, were bred from extremely hardy, prickly roses which grew wild in the British Isles and Europe. They were often referred to as Scotch or Burnet roses. The hybrids have maintained the health and hardiness, and the flowers can be very beautiful, but the bushes are devilishly prickly.

Cécile Brünner 'The Sweetheart Rose' (1881)   Our great-grandmothers loved this rose and so do we. Clusters of tiny, perfectly formed, porcelain pink buds open to fully double, little flowers, ideal for posies, tussiemussies, buttonholes and bedside vases. It is extremely hardy and blooms all summer. The bush form grows to not much more than 1 m, but there is also a very vigorous climbing form. (See Climbers and Ramblers, page 90.)

Corylus (1988)   A cross of *R. rugosa* and

'Fritz Nobis'

R. nitida bred by Hazel Le Rougetel of England, 'Corylus' has all the attributes of an excellent shrub rose and lends itself to mass planting. Big and beautiful silvery pink flowers with pronounced amber stamens are followed by masses of cherry red hips. Foliage is fine and feathery, shiny green on arching branches.

Fritz Nobis (1940)   Dainty but substantial soft pink flowers, deeper at the heart, are clove-scented and charming. The dense bush, which has a little Rugosa in its ancestry for toughness, flowers with great exuberance so that it becomes a mass of soft pink flowers in spring and early summer. It does not repeat bloom, but you will appreciate the display of bright hips in autumn.

Frühlingsanfang (Spring's Opening) (1950)   This Kordes rose's superb big single ivory flowers are wide-eyed harbingers of spring in my garden and I wouldn't be without it. It forms a large, prickly, spring-flowering shrub to more than 2 m, with good autumn colour and hips.

Frühlingsduft (Spring's Fragrance) (1949)   Generous, wide, open double flowers of

'Golden Wings'

apricot and primrose with a strong and heavenly perfume, you will smell this Kordes rose the minute you step into the garden. It has one profuse flowering in spring and it is another tall bush.

Frühlingsgold (Spring's Gold) (1937) Very large, butter yellow flowers, a little more than single, this is again a tall vigorous bush to more than 2 m, but with spring flowering only.

Frühlingsmorgen (Spring Morning) (1942) Another Kordes creation, this offers a delicious perfume in early spring and pretty single flowers that are deep pink around the edges and primrose in the centre. You will get repeat blooms from this one and good autumn hips.

Golden Wings (1956) A well-named and popular rose that flowers repeatedly from early summer through autumn, 'Golden Wings' has big single, butterfly flowers that are golden yellow with prominent amber stamens. Good glossy, soft green foliage on a tall, willowy but thorny shrub.

Grüss an Aachen (1909) Clusters of fat peaches and cream, fully double flowers cover a low growing compact bush. This is the perfect rose to blend in with any colour scheme and to grow at the front of a border.

Horstmann's Rosenresli (1955) Fragrant clusters of pure white double flowers open to show amber stamens. This Kordes creation is a fine, free-flowering Floribunda with glossy foliage and bushy upright growth. It grows to less than 1 m and is an excellent rose for a small garden, as well as making a wonderful long-flowering hedge.

Little White Pet (1879) This is a dear old-rose for a small garden. Clusters of fully double, little white rosettes cover a bushy green plant all summer. It grows to not much more than 75 cm and I have seen it looking superb in a formal garden where it was massed in a long border and edged with clipped box. For a less formal effect, a low-growing lavender, such as 'Hidcote', would have edged it beautifully.

Magenta (1954) This charmer of a rose, opening flat and frilly in clusters, is not the harsh colour of magenta at all, but like no shade I can adequately describe. The best I can do is to say that it opens dusty rose — the colour of old Sanderson linens — and quickly turns to dusty rose dipped in milky coffee: an elegant off-beat faded colour reminiscent of dusty walls in old Italian villas. The bush is tall, strong and healthy and flowers all summer through autumn. It is my favourite modern rose.

Miss Edith Cavell (1917) This rose commemorates a British nursing sister who was executed by a firing squad in Brussels during World War I, on a charge of harbouring British refugees. Rediscovered in a Norfolk garden in 1985 and propagated commercially by Peter Beales' nursery, 'Miss Edith Cavell' is well worth growing. Large clusters of crimson semi-double flowers, with a flash of white in the centre, sit nicely in dark green foliage on a low bush.

Nancy Steen (1976) A New Zealand bred rose named in honour of the author of *The*

'Grüss an Aachen'

'Raubritter'

Charm of Old Roses, its velvet petalled, shapely double blooms are the softest peachy-pink and cream. Abundant flowers begin in summer and end with a generous flush in autumn. The bush is upright and strong.

Raubritter (Macrantha Raubritter) (1936)
In full bloom this rose will stop you in your tracks, so lavish is its display. Clusters of blooms cascade from arching branches, weighing them to the ground. And what blooms they are! Layers of deep pink petals with a pale silvery reverse are cupped to make a plump flowery ball, each petal neatly in place like the feathers on a bird. Blooms cover every part of the low-spreading bush, so that it seems to be a sumptuous flowery mound — a lush outdoor flower arrangement with brandy balloon flowers that hold their shape until they drop. Used as a groundcover, Raubritter is often planted to sprawl over banks, cover tree stumps, or trail prettily near water. English rosarian and author, Hazel Le Rougetel, grows several plants pegged down in a round sunken garden near a door, so that in summer she looks out on a tumbling pool of roses. 'Raubritter' is a superb rose however you choose to grow it, but it flowers only once in summer.

Stanwell Perpetual (1838)   A natural hybrid of a Pimpinellifolia rose and The Autumn Damask, this is a prickly but attractive shrub. Big blush pink, fully double flowers that open flat seem much too delicately pretty for the rugged bush — and what's more, they continue to appear in profusion all summer, making it truly 'perpetual'. Foliage is ferny and flowers are borne all along arching canes. If you want a hardy shrub that flowers forever, this is it. Gertrude Jekyll liked to plant two or three of these roses to create a dense mound.

The Fairy (1941)   Descended from 'Dorothy Perkins', 'The Fairy' has the same big sprays of small fluffy blooms, but they are a gentle pink at their best, although they can look a bit 'lollyish'. It makes a pleasant shrub, hardy and almost always in bloom, and does not get too big. It will flower happily and stay small in a container, and I have seen it used as an ever-blooming and charming hedge.

SHRUB CLIMBERS

These are roses from various families which, for ease of reference, I have grouped together. They are roses with a definite presence, roses that make a bold and beautiful statement in the garden. They will grow to big spreading shrubs and climb if given support. Not one of them will go unnoticed.

Cerise Bouquet (1958) This is a spectacular rose to grow as a specimen shrub in grass if you have a large enough area, or as an ideal woodland rose where it will happily climb trees. Big double, bright cerise flowers cover a great sprawling shrub with arching branches and grey-green foliage. If you have space to spare, grow several bushes in the shrubbery or wild garden. 'Cerise Bouquet' has spring and summer flowering only.

'Ghislaine de Féligonde'

Constance Spry (1961) The ancestor of many of David Austin's English roses, this big beautiful generous rose always reminds me of those lavishly dressed, full-bosomed Edwardian ladies who dallied with Edward VII. A big ungainly sprawling shrub, more of a climber really, 'Constance' will go as high as you let her, arch over, and cascade her blooms down. And what blooms they are! Magnificent full-blown satiny pink 'hat roses' grow in masses in one long triumphant early flowering, all smelling deliciously of myrrh. Let her ramble through a tree or over a fence. This is a oncer, but it is absolutely worth it.

Ghislaine de Féligonde (1916) I have much affection for this hardy and most satisfactory rose which would probably be more popular if it had a shorter name! Although it is classed as a *multiflora* rambler, I'm sure this rose has a dash of Hybrid Musk. It quickly grows to a big arching shrub that will lean against its neighbours in a border or can be trained to climb. Clusters of smallish double flowers are deep orange in the bud, opening apricot and creamy buff. It flowers in two main big flushes in spring and autumn when it can appear more soft pink than apricot. The foliage is tough, glossy and disease-free, and there are very few thorns.

Lavender Lassie (1960) Flat and frilly double, lavender-pink, fragrant flowers in candelabra clusters begin in spring and repeat through summer and autumn. Buds are deep pink and the colour becomes softer and tinged with lavender as the flowers age. Very pretty powder puffs will decorate your garden all summer on a big shrub that can be encouraged to climb. If you want continuous trouble-free flowers with a gentle charm, this is the rose for you. 'Lavender Lassie' is excellent for a pillar or around a doorway.

Maigold (1953) This Pimpinellifolia hybrid from Kordes is a sturdy shrub climber to about 4 m with big double blooms of intense coppery apricot paling to primrose at the edges. An abundantly healthy rose, it is early flowering but not recurrent.

Nevada (1927)   This is the rose that sweeps its big semi-double, creamy-white flowers across trellises and fences, or it can be grown as a big arching shrub if supported. 'Nevada' flowers profusely in spring and early summer with intermittent repeats later, and has bright green leaves and chocolate stems.

Phyllis Bide (1923)   Classed as a Rambler but with strong China/Tea/Noisette influence, this rose was propagated by S Bide & Sons' nursery in Surrey, England and was named after the young daughter of one of the Bide sons. The result of a cross between 'Perle D'Or' and the glorious old Tea rose, 'Gloire de Dijon', 'Phyllis' is a superb rose.

It is difficult to adequately describe the soft blend of colours and the grace of the flower clusters, which are a little like flowers painted on china with the finest of brushes. Bright little buds open to semi-double flowers that are tinted peaches and cream, and pink and primrose, but not obviously or entirely any of those shades. Foliage is small but plentiful and healthy, and the growth is light, airy and easily trained. If you want a big bush or a mannerly climber with non-stop flowers with a delicate air, you cannot do better.

Scarlett Fire (Scharlachglut) (1952)   Scarlet velvet single flowers with golden stamens and sometimes a green eye are highlighted by fresh green foliage, but are not recurrent. However, you get large urn-shaped hips in autumn, and it can be grown as either a big shrub or small climber.

Sea Foam (1964)   Smallish very double, creamy-white blooms with mother-of-pearl buds are like the lacy froth on the seashore. I first saw 'Sea Foam' at the Chelsea Flower Show and immediately wanted it. It makes a spreading, trailing shrub or can be trained to climb, and keeps on flowering through autumn.

'Maigold'

'Phyllis Bide'

CLIMBERS AND RAMBLERS

As the saying goes, 'Who owns the soil, owns up to the sky'. Whatever the size of your garden, you have room for climbers. Walls, fences, arches, pergolas, trellises all look the better for a covering of roses. The smallest townhouse garden will have walls for roses to climb.

Gardening vertically is easy. You can care for 50 climbers in the time it takes to look after the average suburban lawn. The roses mentioned here belong to a variety of families with different characteristics, but for convenience I have grouped them together.

The practical difference between climbers and ramblers is that climbers are bred to go upwards whereas ramblers can easily be trained up but, left to themselves, they will ramble in all directions and can therefore be used to cover banks, tree stumps, and so on. When it comes to pruning, climbers and ramblers are not pruned in the same way. (For pruning advice, refer to Chapter 4.)

Other roses with a climbing habit, notably Bourbons, Noisettes and Hybrid Musks, are described within their family groups or in the Shrub-climber section.

Adélaide d'Orléans (1826) Rambler A very pretty rambler to grow up trees, 'Adélaide's fat cerise buds open to medium-sized double, creamy flowers. The outer petals tinted pink and hang down in clusters like cherry blossom, but there is just one flowering. This rose was bred in the garden of Louis Phillippe, who later became King of France, and it was named after one of his daughters.

Albéric Barbier (1900) Rambler This is a rampantly healthy shiny-leafed evergreen rambler, excellent for a country hedge, or it can be cut back to city limits. The flowers are quite beautiful, opening wide from elegant lemon yellow buds to big loose, muddled double creamy blooms. After one heavy flowering in early summer, it also repeat blooms now and then through the season. Buds, flowers and glossy leaves are perfectly matched.

Albertine (1921) Rambler Everybody loves 'Albertine's loosely double, fragrant, coppery pink blooms borne in profusion. (Vita Sackville-West called them 'tea-coloured', but it must have been rosehip tea.) The plant has one long midsummer flowering and is strong growing but not rampant. It thrives up a tree or over a gazebo.

Alchemist (1956) Climber This has a spectacular flower: big, many-petalled, flat and quartered, a blend of pale creamy gold and country egg-yolk, varying with the season and the weather. 'Alchemist' has one very long and memorable flowering.

Aloha (1949) Climber A sumptuous offspring of the well-known 'New Dawn', 'Aloha' is a better rose than its parent. This fully double rose with an old-fashioned air is clear rose pink with a deeper reverse to the petals — and there are 60 or more to a bloom! A well-mannered climber, it smells divine,

'Aloha'

'American Pillar'

'Adélaide d'Orléans'

begins to flower early and repeats well through the summer. Foliage is healthy, dark and leathery with bronze tints.

American Pillar (1909) Rambler   I like this rose, but don't put it among your *grande dames*. Big, single, vivid pink flowers with a pale centre are borne in clusters. Relentlessly cheerful over a shed or fence, it provides a useful splash of colour on a plant which is very vigorous, thorny and suckering. It has one summer flowering, but the leaves are luxuriant and glossy and colour well in late autumn, when it is prone to mildew.

Apple Blossom (1932) Rambler   A well-named rose with enormous sprays of dainty pink and cream flowers with scalloped edges on a vigorous plant. 'Apple Blossom' is summer flowering only, but it looks lovely combined with a repeat flowering climber on a pergola or rose walk.

Awakening (1935) Climber   Another descendant of 'New Dawn', and the same pale pink but with twice as many petals, fully double and quartered in the old rose style, 'Awakening' is fragrant, floriferous, vigorous, and healthy. This rose arrived in England by chance in the 1980s, in a bundle of cuttings brought back from a Czechoslovakian nursery by an English rosarian on holiday. The cuttings were given to Peter Beales, well known nurseryman and author, who found that one was outstanding and obviously related to 'New Dawn'. The Czechoslovakian name on the label was 'Prubanzeni' which translated to 'Awakening'. By 1990, Peter had built up enough stock to introduce the rose at the Chelsea Flower Show and he donated 10 percent of the takings to a fund for Czechoslavakian orphans.

Bleu Magenta (c.1900) Rambler   Clusters of rich magenta-purple, neatly double flowers fade to parma violet on this shrubby climber with glossy foliage and very few thorns. It is summer flowering only.

Bloomfield Abundance (1920) Climber The vigorous habit of growth and small beautifully formed shell-pink blooms are identical to those of the climbing form of 'Cécile Brünner' and there is often confusion as to which is which. The only difference, really, is that 'Bloomfield Abundance' has long, winged sepals surrounding its buds and 'Cécile Brünner' does not. This is an excellent rose in every way.

Bloomfield Courage (1925) Rambler A mature plant in full bloom is a magnificent sight. Masses of rich, red, small, single flowers with pale centres and gold stamens are borne in big clusters all along the branches. 'Bloomfield' makes an eye-catching splash of colour over an arch, or a superb weeping standard, but it blooms primarily in spring with some repeat flowers later.

Blushing Lucy (1938) Rambler This is a late-blooming rambler, but an enchanting one. Great luscious clusters of scented, clear pink, semi-double flowers with pale centres are flung about in profligate profusion from midsummer through to autumn, when most other ramblers have long since ceased to bloom. The plant is hardy, vigorous, and altogether desirable. 'Blushing Lucy' was bred in England by A H Williams and named for his wife. World War II interrupted the commercial propagation of the rose by Cants of Colchester, and it was not until a son of the breeder returned from the war that one remaining plant was rescued from nursery fields that had been taken over for agriculture. This is definitely high on my list of favourites.

Blush Rambler (1903) Big cascading clusters of pale, powder pink, semi-double cupped flowers are sweetly fragrant and borne on a vigorous plant that will cover a large area. Flowers in early summer.

Bobbie James (1961) Rambler Introduced by English rosarian and author, Graham Thomas, this is a spectacular rambler, but it does need space. Big cascading sprays of fragrant, creamy white flowers with golden stamens probably look their best looping through trees.

Cécile Brünner 'The Sweetheart Rose' (1904) Climbing form No garden should be without this old charmer. Sprays of exquisite porcelain pink little buds and flowers cry out to be picked and put in a posy. A strong, fast-growing bush climber with attrac-tive reddish new growth and fresh green leaves. 'Cécile Brünner' repeat flowers through autumn.

Dorothy Perkins (1901) Rambler Like 'American Pillar', 'Dorothy' is bit blatant and pushy, but the abundant clusters of fluffy little flowers in the brightest fluorescent cerise are cheerful or vulgar depending on your mood. I can't help thinking, though, how she must have brightened the gardens of our great-grandmothers. Good strong foliage early in the season but it will probably mildew after flowering. Plant it near 'American Pillar'. They make good companions and can mildew together.

Dundee Rambler (pre 1850) This is a dense, robust rambler that will cover a sunny bank or envelop a shed in the shade. Big clusters of small, double, milk-white flowers, prettily cupped and with a faint pink blush are borne in summer.

Easlea's Golden Rambler (1932) Yellow ramblers are not thick on the ground — or in the trees — and you won't find a nicer one than 'Easlea's Golden'. Long-stemmed clusters of double flowers are rich golden yellow, leaves are glossy and deeply veined, and growth is vigorous and healthy.

Emily Gray (1918) Rambler Clusters of fragrant, semi-single, buff yellow flowers fading to soft lemon are beautifully offset by glossy foliage, which is plum-coloured when young. Early summer flowering only. Like 'Blushing Lucy', this rose was bred in England by A H Williams and named after a member of his family, this time his sister.

Félicité et Perpétue (1827) Rambler An endearing old rambler that thrives in country hedges, 'Félicité' seems to flower better if left unpruned and to her own devices. Little pink buds open to substantial, round, many-petalled, pearly pompoms in midsummer and there are often repeat blooms. Foliage is large and smooth and inclined to stay on through winter in mild climates. The rose was raised by Antoine Jacques, gardener to the Duke of Orléans, and named after Jacques' twin daughters. The girls had been given the names of Christian martyrs who perished in 203 A.D.

Francis E Lester (1946) Rambler This is a well-mannered rambler with moderate growth, suitable for a small garden. Pleasantly citrus-scented blooms are semi-double, ivory white touched with pink, and open to show bright gold stamens. Leaves are large, smooth and plentiful on a summer-flowering rambler well worth growing.

Francois Juranville (1906) Rambler English rosarian Peter Beales calls this rose 'a refined Albertine' and it is just that. The colour is a little gentler and the flowers are a little more relaxed and gracious. In vigour, form, and blooming habit it resembles the remarkable 'Albertine'.

Gardenia (1899) Rambler Long pointed pale yellow buds open to full, deliciously muddled, big flat flowers of creamy white with a touch of yellow in the centres. An apple fragrance and one long mid-summer flowering for this treasure, 'Gardenia' has a vigorous plant with glossy leaves.

Gerbe Rose (1904) Climber A rose of refinement, 'Gerbe Rose' has big, loosely double, soft pink flowers, which are sometimes quartered. They are fragrant and beautiful in a gentle way. Primarily summer flowering, but with frequent repeats, this is a rose that lends itself to training on a pillar.

Goldfinch (1907) Rambler From deep yellow buds, flowers open primrose and show rich amber stamens as the petals pale. Airy flowers among shining green leaves on a well behaved, almost thornless plant of moderate growth make this an ideal rambler for a small garden. It only flowers once though.

Hiawatha (1904) Rambler Clusters of small single, cerise-crimson flowers with a distinct white eye are like a smaller version

'Francis E Lester'

of 'American Pillar'. A vigorous plant, 'Hiawatha' flowers for a long time in summer.

Kew Rambler (1912) Rambler Bearing massive clusters of soft pink flowers with pale centres and bronze stamens, the rose's individual blooms are quite large for a rambler and very fragrant. With grey-green foliage and abundant flowers in summer, this is a lovely rambler to decorate a white picket fence.

'Gerbe Rose'

'May Queen'

Lauré Davoust (1843) Rambler A very old rambler and the first one I grew — I have a lot of affection for this rose with its many-petalled lilac pink flowers which open flat and quartered to show a green eye. It blooms only once but you will enjoy it. I have seen it grown with 'Climbing Cécile Brünner' and the two old charmers go beautifully together.

Léontine Gervais (1903) Rambler Big loose flowers are an interesting mix of coppery pink and deep gold. 'Léontine's growth is strong but slender, and foliage is dark and glossy.

Lorraine Lee (1932) Climber Bred from a seedling of the Burmese *R. gigantea* by Alistair Clark of Australia, 'Lorraine Lee' has inherited vigorous growth habits, smooth stems and long luxuriant leaves. I am very fond of this rose. Although the blooms are large and loosely double, they have the charm of a wild rose and a fresh, almost herbal, fragrance. The colour is difficult to describe. The luscious pink of watermelon, lit by a yellow glow at the base of each delicately veined petal, is the best I can do. In its hometown of Melbourne, 'Lorraine Lee' is capable of flowering all year and makes the most enchanting hedge. Given a warm situation, in temperate climates it could certainly manage a very long flowering indeed. Cut it back in autumn for winter flowers if your winters are not too harsh.

May Queen (1898) Rambler This is an underrated rose. After a flush of flowers in early summer, it repeats intermittently and you can almost always pick a pretty, crumpled, muddled double bloom, deep pink at the centre and paling on the outside. The healthy, glossy leaves often stay on all winter. It will form a very large sprawling mound, useful for covering banks and tree stumps. or it can be trained over a fence to form a hedge. 'May Queen' grows rapidly, so allow it plenty of space.

Minnehaha (1905) Rambler A vigorous and beautiful rambler, 'Minnehaha' has big clusters of fluffy double flowers that can be richest rose-madder, but fade to a paler pink. I have seen this rose grown over a pergola where its long lush clusters hung down like rose-tinted grapes. Plant it in a warm sheltered spot and expect repeat flowers.

'New Dawn'

'Nancy Hayward'

Nancy Hayward (1937) Climber This is another superb climber bred from *R. gigantea* by Alistair Clark of Australia. 'Nancy' is a wonderfully flamboyant, yet elegant, rose whose big lipstick scarlet, single blooms are all of 12.5 cm across. It's a vigorous, spectacular rose for growing up trees, but remember that it was bred in Australia and does need a reasonably warm spot. I once saw it high above a tree-lined driveway, looped from tree to tree like Christmas lights. It is capable of flowering all season.

New Dawn (1930) Climber This glossy-leaved climber with double, pale pink blooms has become extremely popular in the last few years, partly because it repeat flowers. It grows strongly and flowers prolifically in early summer, then repeats throughout the season, but don't expect that first fine careless rapture. Although it is reported to be fragrant, I cannot detect much perfume. I don't mean to damn it with faint praise as it is a worthwhile rose, but I am fonder of its progeny, 'Awakening' and 'Aloha'.

Paul Transon (1900) Rambler The flowers of this rose are large for a rambler, with concentric rows of pointed petals shorter in the centre, almost like a dahlia — although sometimes it is so full of petals that it is raggedy. From coppery buds, the flowers open a soft washed terracotta pink, deeper in the centre. A fast-growing, healthy plant with shiny leaves, 'Paul Transon' repeat flowers intermittently though summer and often gives a good autumn display.

Pierre de Ronsard (1987) Climber Yes, the date of introduction is 1987, not 1897, and this is a modern, French-bred rose, but I have to include it because any lover of old roses would give their eye teeth for it. Voluptuous is the word — a big, soft, sumptuous, consistently globular rose, ivory on the outside deepening to centre petals of dusty rose. Musk rose fragrance, a profusion of flowers, and very few thorns, are further points in its favour. It makes a heavenly pillar rose, but like many fat full-petalled roses, it dislikes wet weather. The real Pierre de Ronsard was the French poet who wrote so prettily and often about roses — and love, of course.

Rambling Rector 'Shakespeare's Musk' Ancient Rambler A rampant vigorous rambler, this rose is wonderful for growing up trees or covering sheds and large pergolas. Enormous clusters of fragrant double white flowers with bright gold stamens bloom in midsummer.

'Minnehaha'

'Wedding Day'

Rose Marie Viaud (1924) Rambler A seedling of the better known 'Veilchenblau', 'Rose Marie Viaud' bears clusters of rosettes in cerise purple fading to lilac mauve. She is a vigorous rambler with light green leaves and few thorns.

Sanders White (1912) Rambler A reliable hardy rambler with light green foliage, 'Sanders White' has cascading clusters of little white rosettes with a fruity fragrance. Its growth is pliable and easily trained, and the rose is often sold as a weeping standard.

Seagull (1907) Rambler This 'Seagull' will happily perch in trees or swoop up walls. Bright yellow stamens and layers of white petals are borne in big, airy, scented clusters in early summer.

Silver Moon (1910) A *R. laevigata* hybrid which is well named, this rampant rose will rapidly reach the top of trees and shine down on you. Big, butterfly-like, single flowers are ivory and white with golden stamens and the foliage is dark and glossy. It has one long summer flowering, but don't expect a mass of blooms. You will have to gaze upwards for a while.

Tausendschön (Thousand Beauties) (1906) Rambler Loose clusters of double flowers that vary from rose-pink to blush, touched with white in the centre, are borne on long graceful stems with very few thorns. It flowers prolifically and looks spectacular. If you deadhead, this rose will repeat but not with the generosity of its first blooming.

Tea Rambler (1904) Another lovely Edwardian rambler, this rose has quite large soft pink, full and fragrant flowers. A healthy rose with glossy foliage, it flowers for a long time in spring and you get repeat blooms later.

Veilchenblau (Violet Blue) (1909) Rambler Not a blue rose, thankfully, but it has clusters of small flowers that range in colour from the deepest violet through rosy lilac to lavender grey, with a white highlight in the centre and yellow stamens. This vigorous healthy rambler is a memorable sight in full bloom. I have seen it looking spectacular trained horizontally against a wall and underplanted with tall toning fuchsias. You get one long summer flowering normally, but sheep ate my 'Veilchenblau' last year towards the end of its flowering and it bloomed again! This year I will cut it back and see what happens.

Wedding Day (1950) Rambler Another popular rampant rambler, 'Wedding Day' festoons trees and flings itself over pergolas and arbours. Clusters of big, single, ivory white flowers with prominent yellow stamens are beautifully offset by fresh, green, glossy leaves. A strong grower with few thorns, it has only one flowering in summer.

BIBLIOGRAPHY

Austin, David. *Old Roses and English Roses*. Antique
    Collectors' Club, 1991

Beales, Peter. *Classic Roses*. Collins Harvill, 1985

Beales, Peter. *Twentieth Century Roses*. Collins Harvill,
    1988

Biddle, Violet. *Roses and How to Grow Them*.
    C. Arthur Pearson Ltd, London, 1906

Biddle, Violet. *Small Gardens and How to Make the Most
    of Them*. C. Arthur Pearson Ltd, London, c.1900

Borchard, Ruth. *Oh My Own Rose*. Published by the
    author, Switzerland, c.1980.

Blunt, Wilfred & Russel J. *Old Garden Roses, Pt.2*.
    George Rainbird, 1957

Ellwanger, Henry B. *The Rose*. William Heinemann,
    London, 1893

Fisher, John. *The Companion to Roses*. Viking, 1986

Foster-Melliar A. *The Book of the Rose*. Macmillan & Co.
    Ltd., 1894

Gibson, Michael. *Shrub roses, Climbers and Ramblers*.
    William Collins, Sons & Co., London

Griffiths, Trevor. *My World of Old Roses, Vol.1*.
    Whitcoulls, 1987

Hole, S. Reynolds. *A Book About Roses*. Edward Arnold
    Ltd, 1869

Jekyll, Gertrude. *Home and Garden*. Longmans Green &
    Co., 1900

Jekyll, Gertrude and Morley, Edward. *Roses for English
    Gardens*. Republished by Antique Collectors' Club,
    1982

Johnson, Hugh. *The Principles of Gardening*. Mitchell
    Beazley Publishers Ltd, 1979

Le Rougetel, Hazel. *A Heritage of Roses*. Unwin Hyman,
    London, 1989

Lindsay, Nancy. *The Shrub Rose List*. Published by author,
    1955

Money, Keith. *The Bedside Book of Old-fashioned Roses*.
    Degamo Productions U.K. Ltd, 1985

Pratt, Nigel. *Old Garden Roses in Summer*. Published by
    author, 1992

Rohde, Eleanor Sinclair. *Rose Recipes from Olden Times*.
    Dover Publications, 1973

Ross, Dean M. *A Manual of Heritage Roses*. Published by
    author, 1989

Sinclair, Alan & Thodey, Rosemary. *Gardening with Old
    Roses*. Godwit Press, 1993

Sitwell, S. & Russell, J. *Old Garden Roses, Pt.1*. George
    Rainbird, 1955

Steen, Nancy. *The Charm of Old Roses*. A.H. & A.W.
    Reed, 1966

Thomas, G.S. *The Old Shrub Roses*. Phoenix House, 1955

Journals of Heritage Roses Societies of New Zealand,
    Australia, England and U.S.A.

INDEX

'Adelaide d'Orleans' 88, *89*
'Agnes' 69
'Aimée Vibert' 66
'Alain Blanchard' 41
Alba Semi-plena 17
'Albéric Barbier' 16, 88
'Albertine' *9, 25*, 88
'Alchemist' *9, 26*, 88
'Alfred de Dalmas' 53
'Alister Stella Gray' 66
'Allen Chandler' 76
'Aloha' 88, *88*
'American Pillar' 89, *89*
'Anaïs Ségalas' 41, *41*
'Anna Marie de Montraval' 13, 56
'Anna Pavlova' 17, 73
aphids 33
'Apple Blossom' 89
'Autumn Delight' 11, 80
'Awakening' 89
'Ballerina' *6, 79*, 80
Banksia 16
bare root roses 20, 23
'Baron Girod de L'Ain' 71
'Baroness Rothschild' 71
'Baronne Henriette de Snoy' 74
'Baronne Prévost' 71
'Belle Amour' 48
'Belle de Crécy' 42
'Belle Isis' 42
'Belle Poitevine' 69
black spot 34, 35
'Blanc Double de Coubert' 17, 69, *69*
'Blanchefleur' 51
'Bleu Magenta' 89

'Bloomfield Abundance' 89
'Bloomfield Courage' 90
'Bloomfield Dainty' 80
blooming 14
'Blush Rambler' 90
'Blushing Lucy' 90
'Bobbie James' 90
'Bon Silene' 74
'Boule de Neige' 61
'Bouquet d'Or' 66
'Bourbon Queen' 61, *61*
budding 30
'Buff Beauty' *10*, 11, 80, *80*
'Camaieux' 42
Canary Bird 37, *37*
'Capitaine John Ingram' 53
'Cardinal de Richelieu' 42
'Catherine Mermet' 74
'Cécile Brünner' 83
    climbing form *19*, 90
'Celestial' 48
'Céline Forestier' *29*, 66
'Celsiana' 47
'Cerise Bouquet' 86
'Chapeau de Napoléon' 53, *53*
'Charles de Mills' 14, 42, *42*
'Chislaine de Féligonde' 86
'Chloris' 48
'Claire Jacquier' 66
climbers 12, 25, 76, 88
'Cloth of Gold' 66
'Clytemnestra' 80
'Commandant Beaurepaire' 62
companion plants 17, 18
'Complicata' 43, *43*

compost 26
'Comte de Chambord' 59, *59*
'Comtesse de Murinais' 53
'Comtesse du Cayla' 56
'Conrad Ferdinand Meyer' 69
'Constance Spry' 86
container-grown roses 22, 24
containers 13
'Cornelia' 11, *22*, 81
'Corylus' 83
'Coupe d'Hébé' 62
'Crépuscule' *1*, 66, *67*
'Cupid' 76
cuttings 30, 31, 32
'Dainty Bess' *73*, 74
'Danae' 81
deadheading 29
'Devoniensis' 76
'Dorothy Perkins' 90
downy mildew 34
'Duc de Guiche' 43
'Duchesse d'Angoulême' 43
'Duchesse de Brabant' 74
'Duchesse de Montebello' 15, 43
'Dundee Rambler' 14, 90
'Easlea's Golden Rambler' 90
'Ellen Willmott' 74
'Emily Gray' 90
'Empress Josephine' 8, 43
'Eugénie Guinoisseau' 54, *54*
'Fantin-Latour' 17, 51, *51*
feeding 26
'Felicia' 11, *21*
'Félicité et Perpétue' 90
'Félicité Parmentier' 48

'Ferdinand Pichard' 71, *71*
fertiliser 26
'Fortune's Double Yellow' 76
fragrance 16
'Francesca' 81
'Francis E Lester' 91, *91*
'Francois Juranville' 91
'Frau Karl Druschki' 71
'Fritz Nobis' 16, 83, *83*
'Fru Dragmar Hastrup' 70
'Frühlingsanfang' 83
'Frühlingsduft' 17, 83
'Frühlingsgold' 16, 84
'Frühlingsmorgen' 84
'Gardenia' 91
'General Gallieni' 74
'General Jacqueminot' 71
'Général Kléber' 54
Geranium 38
'Gerbe Rose' 91, *91*
'Ghislaine de Féligonde' 86, *86*
'Gloire de Dijon' 77
'Gloire de Mousseux' 54
'Golden Wings' 84, *84*
'Goldfinch' 91
'Grace Darling' 74, *75*
ground-covering roses 14
'Grüss an Aachen' 13, 84, *85*
'Grüss an Teplitz' 56, *57*
'Guinée' 77
'Hansa' 70
hardwood cuttings 32
heeling in new plants 22
'Hermosa' 13, 57
'Hiawatha' 91
'Hippolyte' 44, *44*
'Honorine de Brabant' 62, *62*
'Horstmanns Rosenresli' 84
humus 26
'Ipsilanté' 44
'Irène Watts' 57
'Ispahan' 46, 47
'Jacques Cartier' 15, 60, *60*
'James Veitch' 54
'Jaune Desprez' 66
'Jean Ducher' *17*, 74, *75*
'Jeanne d'Arc' 48
'Jeanne de Montfort' 54
'Jenny Duval' 44
'Juno' 52
'Kathleen Harrop' 62
'Kazanlik' 17, 47
'Kew Rambler' 91
'Kiftsgate' 38
'La Belle Sultane' 44
'La France' 75
'La Noblesse' 52
'La Reine Victoria' 62
'La Ville de Bruxelles' 47
'Lady Curzon' 70
'Lady Hillingdon' 77, *77*
'Lady Waterlow' 77
'Lamarque' 17, 66
landscaping with roses
  beds 10
  borders 10
  in grass 11
  in woodland 11
'Lauré Davoust' 92
'Lavender Lassie' 86
layering 32
'Léda' *47*, 47
'Léontine Gervais' 92
'Little White Pet' 84
'Lorraine Lee' 92
'Louis XIV' 57
'Louise Odier' 62
'Magenta' 84
'Magnifica' 70
'Maiden's Blush' 17, 49
'Maigold' 86, *87*

'Maréchal Davoust' 54
'Maréchal Niel' 68
'Marie de Blois' 54
'Marie Louise' 47
'Max Graf' 14, 70
'Maxima' 49
'May Queen' 14, 92, *92*
'Meg' 77
'Mermaid' 39
'Minnehaha' *13*, 92, *93*
'Miss Edith Cavell' 84
'Mme Alfred Carrière' 67, *67*
'Mme Caroline Testout' 77, *77*
'Mme de la Roche-Lambert' 54
'Mme Ernst Calvat' *3*, 62, 63
'Mme Grégoire Staechelin' 78
'Mme Hardy' 47
'Mme Isaac Pereire' 17, 63, *63*
'Mme Jules Graveraux' 78
'Mme Laurette Messimy' 57
'Mme Lauriol de Barny' *8*, 63, *63*
'Mme Legras de St Germain' 17, 49, *49*
'Mme Louis Lévêque' 54, *55*
'Mme Pierre Oger' 64
'Mme Plantier' 49, *49*
'Moonlight' 81
'Mrs Anthony Waterer' 70
'Mrs John Lang' 72
'Mrs Oakley Fisher' 75
mulching 26
'Mutabilis' 11, 58, *58*
'Nancy Hayward' 93, *93*
'Nancy Steen' 84
'Nestor' 44
'Nevada' 87
'New Dawn' *92*, 93
nourishing 26
'Nozomi' 14
'Nuits de Young' 55
'Old Blush' *5*, 58, *58*
'Omar Khayyam' 48
'Ophelia' 75
organic rose spray 34
'Paul Neyron' 72
'Paul Ricault' 72
'Paul Transon' 93
'Paul's Lemon Pillar' 78
'Peace' 75, 76
pegging a rose 11
'Pélisson' 55
'Penelope' 11, *21*, 81, *81*
'Perle d'Or' 13
pests 33
'Petite de Hollande' 52
'Petite Lisette' 52
'Phyllis Bide' *18*, 87, *87*
'Pierre de Ronsard' 93
planting 22, 24
potting medium 31
powdery mildew 34, 35
'Prince Camille de Rohan' 72
propagation 30
'Prosperity' 82
pruning 28, 30
  climbers 28
  once-flowering roses 28
  ramblers 29
  repeat-flowering roses 28
'Queen of Denmark' 50, *50*
R. banksiae alba plena 36, *36*
R. banksiae lutea 37, *37*
R. bracteata 37
R. brunonii 37
R. canina 37
R. centifolia 51
R. centifolia muscosa 53
R. damascena bifera 46
R. dupontii 15, 37
R. eglanteria 8, 38
R. fedtschenkoana 38
R. foetida bicolor 38, *39*
R. foliolosa 16

R. fortuniana 38
R. gallica officinalis 40
R. gallica versicolor 40
R. glauca 16, 38
R. helenae 38, *38*
R. laevigata 39
R. longicuspis 39
R. moyesii 16
R. omeiensis pteracantha 16
R. pimpinellifolia 16
R. roxburghii 16
R. roxburghii plena 39
R. rugosa alba 68, 69
R. woodsii fendlerii 16
'Rambling Rector' 93
'Raubritter' 14, 85, *85*
red spider mite 33, 34
'Reine des Violettes' 72, *72*
'Reve d'Or' 68
'Robert le Diable' 52, *52*
Rosa Mundi 40, *41*
'Rose de Rescht' 60, *60*
'Rose du Maître d'Ecole' 44
'Rose du Roi' 60
'Rose Marie Viaud' 94
rose sickness 23
rosehips 16
'Roseraie de l'Hay' *23*, 70, *70*
'Rosette Delizy' 76
Rugosa alba 16, *16*
rust 35
'Sadlers Wells' 82
'Safrano' 78
'Sanders White' 94
'Scabrosa' 70
'Scarlett Fire' 87
'Sea Foam' 14, 87
'Seagull' 94
'Semi-plena' 50
'Shot Silk' 76
'Silver Moon' 94
'Snow Carpet' 14
soil 23, 26
'Sombreuil' 78
'Sophie's Perpetual' 59
'Souvenir de la Malmaison' *7*, 17, 64
'Souvenir de Mme Léonie Viennot' 78
'Souvenir de Philémon Cochet' 70
'Souvenir de St Annes' 64, *64*
'Souvenir du Docteur Jamain' 72
'Souvenir d'un Ami' *78*, 79
spraying 35
'Stanwell Perpetual' 85
suckers 31
'Sweet Briar' 8
'Tausendschön' 94
'Tea Rambler' 94
'The Bishop' 52
'The Fairy' 13, 85
'Thérèse Bugnet' 16
'Tour de Malakoff' 52, *52*
transplanting 25, 26
'Tricolore de Flandre' 44, *45*
'Trier' 82
'Tuscany' 44
'Tuscany Superb' 45
'Vanity' 82
'Variegata di Bologna' 64
'Veilchenblau' 94
'Vick's Caprice' 72
'Village Maid' 53
water 26
'Wedding Day' 94, *94*
weeds 26
white scale 34
'Wilhelm' 82, *82*
'William Lobb' 55
willow tea 31
winter spray programme 35
'Zéphirine Drouhin' 64, *65*